# VOX

## The New Avant Garde

# #3
# 2007

# CONTENTS

# CONTENTS

VOX
The New Avant Garde

EDITORS
LOUIS E. BOURGEOIS
J. E. PITTS
BOOK REVIEWER
TOM PYNN
PUBLICIST
ANNA BAKER
DESIGN
J. E. PITTS
PRINTING
BOOKMOBILE, INC.

VOX (ISSN: 1553-7242) is published once a year by VOX Press, Inc. Founded in 2004 by Louis E. Bourgeois, Max Bishop Hipp, and J. E. Pitts. Issues available for $6.00. Editorial address: P.O. Box 527, Oxford, MS 38655. Email submissions are welcome at *submit@voxjournal.com*. For email and postal mail submissions send no more than 3-5 pages of text in any genre. Postal manuscripts must be accompanied by a self-addressed stamped envelope for a response. Newly published or forthcoming poetry collections may be sent to the editorial address for possible review. Requests for special permission and reprint rights should be directed to Vox Press. POSTMASTER: Send address changes to VOX, P. O. Box 527, Oxford, MS 38655. All rights reserved. Copyright 2007 by Vox Press, Inc. Rights revert to author upon publication.

mississippi arts commission
support inspire enrich

yoknapatawpha

arts council

THANKS TO THE
MISSISSIPPI ARTS COMMISSION AND
THE YOKNAPATAWPHA ARTS
COUNCIL FOR THEIR SUPPORT OF VOX.

*VOX*
is
distributed
by
**Bernard Deboer,
Inc.**

*VOX*

**POETRY**

**PROSE**

**REVIEWS**

**TRANSLATIONS**

**INTERVIEWS**

**LINKS**

**BACK ISSUES**

**ARCHIVE**

WWW.VOXJOURNAL.COM

# we must become absolutely modern

### -Rimbaud

# ANNA BAKER

## THERE IS NO FUNERAL WITHOUT LAUGHING, NO WEDDING WITHOUT BREAD

*(from Transylvania Diaries)*.

For dinner we ate cut slabs of pig fat off a pig hanging in an old safe in a woman's barn. It was her way of keeping the meat cold. We put pig fat on sticks and held it over an outside fire in the orchard; we let the fat drip onto our pieces of bread. This was our meal. When it was over our history teacher urinated on the fire. He wore a pink shirt with an orange sweater. His wife died last week. Before she died, he was the sharpest dresser. My first night in Transylvania, the full moon first orange, then white and the lands that were flat became the Carpathian Mountains. We were a busload of Europeans, Americans and the history teacher. There is a French man on the floor in the next room. Wonderful night, still and dark, except for the light.

Cow with wings carved on the church.

The forest cleared in medieval times brings erosion now.

Just went to the sheep market in another town where they butchered the lambs right on the spot. The lambs were tied by their feet or bought alive. Some of the lambs bought live were tied by their feet and hung upside down, carried home by men on bikes, the lambs hanging upside down on the handlebars.

A father, dark skinned Romanian, well dressed in front of the church, catches a pigeon with his hands, and then calls over two little children. When they are standing in front of him, he lets go, it flies furious and clumsily away from them in the hot sun. The church people are setting up old plastic microphones facing in all directions, open mouths in all directions to tell the people something.

Last night was Orthodox Easter. I came here to Sekely to the church for the small Romanian population in this village of 4,000 Hungarians. The service had the spirit of God in it, unlike most places. I walked with a bent over old woman in black around the church three times looking for the body of Christ. Then the preacher in whitish tan robes took a wooden cross and banged on the wooden door of the stone church. (Graves are all around the church, many of them new.) They are not buried in any particular order. The door opened and the man inside told us that Christ has risen.

6

There are two witches in the village. Woman and daughter.

In the protestant church the preacher stands under his own wooden roof where a pelican is carved, baby birds suckle its belly.

Each generation wears the fashion of their youth for the rest of their lives. The men my age are wearing Members Only jackets with work boots and wool hats.

When a woman has a baby girl she starts making her linens and clothes for the whole baby's life. First the basic stuff like sheets or pillowcases in case the child dies. Then more delicate shirts some worth 2,000, but nobody has that kind of money. Somewhere it is worth so much. The old woman says that here untouchable riches are more valuable than money.

We went to the peasant celebration of the milking of sheep. They are brought from the hills and milked, whichever family has ewe with the most milk, gains prestige for a year. Why not forget everything, but the way the hills rolled and the people came from the churches in their costumes? The pearl headdresses for the virgins. The black knee-high boots every woman wore. The black scarves around the old women's heads.

A whole town of only stone carvers, every son born becomes a stone carver.

There was an old man in his studio, two of his fingers were cut off. He stood in the middle of his dark stone room. One wall is all statues carved from a single rock of Christ teaching the women, all their faces facing his direction. The artist never took his good hand from the lamb he was carving that day. I knew it was a lamb even before he told us.

All gypsy towns have silver roofs on the buildings and the walls are covered with enlarged photos of sunsets on beaches. Or of foggy forests, this is their wallpaper.

All the roads are dirt. All the villages close together in close settlement patterns, and built in valleys so they were protected from the Tartars and the Mongols. When I walked into the hills, I could see the Tartars coming, like in the old times. There was nowhere to hide, nowhere to go. They were the people on the horses, valuing only that that could be carried or what could walk or ride a horse. They were coming from the East, riding west toward Spain. I wanted to go with them. I have always preferred the horse over bread.

# GISÈLE PRASSINOS
*(translated from the French by Margot Miller)*

## NEIGE

Il paraît que le ciel et la terre
Vont se marier.
Avant l'aube le fiancé
Sur la fille
A jeté son voile de mousse
Lentement et sans bruit
Pour ne pas l'éveiller.

Elle sommeille encore il est tôt
mais déjâ exaltés
impatients d'aller à la noce
les arbres ont mis leurs gants
par milliers
et les maisons leurs chapeaux blancs.

## SNOW

It seems the sky and the earth
are getting married.
Before dawn the bridegroom
over the maiden
has thrown his veil of froth
slowly and noiselessly
so as not to wake her.

She sleeps it is still early
but already exalted and
impatient to go to the wedding
the trees have put on their gloves
by the thousands
and the houses their white hats.

## LA LUNE A FROID

La lune a froid
La lune a peur
La lune est seule.

Comme tout le monde n'a-t-elle pas
appris dans les livres d'astronomie
combine les étoiles sont lointaines?

## THE MOON IS COLD

The moon is cold
The moon is afraid
The moon is alone.

Why hasn't she, like everyone else
learned in astronomy books
how far away the stars are?

## DANS TES YEUX IL Y LA MER

Dans tes yeux il y a la mer.
Sur la mer il y a la tempête.
Dans la tempête : une barque.
Dans la barque : une petite fille.
Dans la petite fille il y a ton enfant
et je vais me noyer maman
si tu ne cesses de gronder.

## IN YOUR EYES THERE IS THE OCEAN

In your eyes there is the ocean.
On the Ocean there is a storm.
In the storm : a ship.
In the ship : a little girl.
In the little girl there is your child
and I am going to drown, Mama
if you don't stop scolding.

# THE PSYCHE

My husband, who traveled a lot for business, had given me that year as a Christmas gift a *psyche*, the kind of standing mirror that can be tilted to see the whole body. It's true that for a long time I'd pretend to complain that I could never see my whole self, except in shop windows. I didn't know myself except from the waist up, the image the living room mirror above the fireplace, gave me. Even in childhood, I'd only ever seen myself as an upper torso.

I didn't tell anyone but I had an idea of my full appearance, thanks not to the mirror but to another human being who looked like me. I know, a mirror offers almost scientific proof while a human being offers only an image subject to interpretation, which is suppose to me more like poetry.

The day the *psyche* was delivered, I hesitated to look at myself. I was a little tired, I wanted to wait until I felt better, wanted to put on make-up and to protect myself a little. Still, I was all the more impatient to discover my exact totality, of which I had an inkling and because I was six months pregnant. There is a tendency to put off pleasure as much as disappointment.

Late one afternoon, imagining, imagining an exceptional outing, I dressed in anticipation. I was alone in the house and took pleasure in the solemnity of the occasion as I approached my full-length portrait. I moved toward the oval mirror with my eyes closed and my hands outstretched, like a blind person. My fingers met and recognized the carved, copper frame, traced the relief of its engraving: a design of leaves. I stepped back and waited again.

When I opened my eyes, I didn't even look at my belly. SHE was behind me, HER, my double, my thief.

We met for the first time four years ago, in a bakery. I was behind her in line. She was paying for a loaf of white bread. "Are you together?" asked the clerk. "No. No..." "You look alike," she said again. We looked at each other pleasantly, the other and I. I'd chosen a country-style loaf and was looking for change in my bag when I heard, "Give me a country loaf instead..." We went out together, walked a short distance in concert, and I showed her where I lived.

To tell the truth, at the time, we were still different. Yes, the same height, the same shape face. Her blonde hair was cut in a Joan-of-Arc cut whereas mine was dark, flowing softly over my shoulders. She wore dresses and skirts. I preferred slacks and sweaters.

She got in the habit of coming to my house without being invited. I didn't complain. I was curious about the changes that came over her physical aspect. First, she colored her hair the same color as mine and let it grow out. Then she started using the same make-up and began dressing in my more masculine style.

Was it a reaction or did she earn it by imitation — albeit slowly — the way I passed her the baton? The following summer, I bought a red cotton dress, tight at the waist, and black high-heeled shoes. Two days later, she was wearing the exact same outfit when she arrived at the house and I remember that we stood looking at each other a moment in silence, each watching the other's slightest gesture, the way one looks at oneself in the mirror, replacing a strand of hair or buttoning up a coat. Then, looking into each other's eyes, we smiled, shyly. I was troubled. She triumphant, probably, I don't know how, but it brought us closer.

My nature is unpredictable and I'm likely to change my mind from one minute to the next. With respect to my visitor, I went constantly from exasperation to compassion. Thus, annoyed one day, I thought about changing my lipstick and eye shadow. That very evening, I decided. I worried about upsetting my friend, about letting her know that her incessant efforts to mimic me were getting on my nerves. Was it really a question of effort? I was less and less sure. Then it occurred to me that a powerful instinct for self preservation was forcing her to take over my being in order to fill in a void in herself that threatened to drag her toward Nothingness. So she was not my responsibility and my hands were tied.

Because, once she had adopted my clothing style, the color of my hair, the brand of my make-up and even the cadence of my steps, the way I ate and the smallest of my mannerisms, a new period had started. She took over suddenly, without transition, without so much as a nuanced suggestion, such as even an industrial machine that's going from one phrase of production to another must.

She began to speak. Up until then, she had uttered only yeses and nos, onomatopoeias and echoes. She began to speak, that is, she let go a stream of words and then stopped abruptly. She started again. Her discourse was more focused and I recognized, not without tightening in my chest, the sound of my voice, my favorite ways of saying things and my pet terms, even my pauses for reflection. The next day, it was perfect. If I closed my eyes, it seemed I was listening to myself on a tape recording. I didn't have the courage to speak. After hearing her, I felt heavy with silence, my brain evacuated, dispossessed. When I was conscious again, I didn't think of taking myself back. I accepted this theft with all the rest. The following week, when we started to converse, it was the same. We had become more than twins and we each saw the other, subjected, in the human mirror we each held for the other.

I began to read assiduously as a way of holding on to my mind, of getting new ideas, new sensations, as a way of fortifying myself in advance against her appetite. She could no longer follow me. One evening, I was looking for the book I was reading, which I always kept next to my bed. It had disappeared and I put it down to recent difficulties with my memory. I also knew the ease with which I used to speak had of late turned to a rough cadence, painfully consigning thoughts to clichés. I must have moved the book in my distraction, I didn't know where. When I lost a second, and then a third, it occurred to me that SHE had taking them without asking. My energy left me. I was conscious of a change in myself. But had neither the desire nor the power to do anything about it.

Shortly thereafter, her reflection confirmed that I was not mistaken. She subtly analyzed the books in question, shamelessly, with so precise and clear a vocabulary that I was impressed with my friend. I was giving up.

This friend...But I knew nothing about her. Where she came from, married or single, her last name, all of it was a mystery, not to mention her address and even her first name. I asked her finally. "Baptize me," she responded. "How about Pandora, if you like it..." "No, the same as you." "Louise, then?" "Louise."

I thought she was marvelous, brilliant. She put on a bit of weight and the taut skin on her face, forehead and cheeks, bore the soft light of winter sunshine.

And me? Who? What? I lost weight, emptied myself out. I was languid and my weakness approved of everything without consulting myself. At the same time, a strange tremor inhabited me, which I couldn't control let alone name.

When I stopped speaking and eating altogether, my family, very worried, made the decision to take me to the doctor, who recommended a long rest at a sanatorium. I don't remember this cure. As soon as I arrived at the clinic I must have forgotten why I was there and, as a result, the existence of the other Louise.

Today, I think, SHE took me over little by little, over the course of two years, until she had enriched herself with my mental and physical substances, leaving me with only what she herself was. The exchange and its effect had happened. We crossed swords and I had lost.

A year later, thanks to the prescribed treatment far away from what had threatened me, my body recovered its strength and its former faculties, including memory, enough to light the darkest night.

On this late afternoon, eight months after my return home, I stood in front of the *psyche* which I had decided to approach with my eyes closed. I had hardly opened them when I SAW HER behind me, framed inside the copper oval of finely carved leaves. I recognized her, but with difficulty, as if she had come out of a former life that I had lived under a form I no longer knew. At first only a thin pencil line, SHE slowly came into focus, whereas I, from head to toe for the first time, began to shiver in total physical fear, intimidated, face to face with this undone, ashen, gaunt being. It took me a few seconds to place her, and guided by the horror I felt, to fight off a flood of compassion.

How had she gotten it? And suddenly I wondered how she had gotten in everyday before. The room was lit by a small neon tube, under which I had placed the mirror so that the *psyche* was practically glowing. It was in this intensity that the other Louise, after noting the elegance of my attire, directed her eyes at my belly, a long time, with a look of terror, beaten, which I took to be a reproach. Then she turned away and I saw her slowly, go away, melt, disappear in the half-light of my bedroom. Soon she was not behind me any more, or anywhere at all.

I hadn't seen the door open, and I didn't hear it close.

# FINDING WITHOUT LOOKING

My poor daughter has a man's voice, a male filament that has invaded her throat.

"I have up my sleeve," she says, "some lovely intoxicating faces, just what you need."

And she searches, poor girl, assiduously, while our clients run away, frightened, their ears disturbed and already aching.

And my daughter calls out and gives up.

"Stop your crying, poor thing." I say while patting her, "We'll go see the surgeon to get a real woman's voice."

Just then, a handsome young man comes by and nods at us. He stops and asks something. His voice is frail and soft, we don't understand him.

"Serene, innocent, cunning faces," says my poor daughter trying to make herself smaller. And she hides her tears so as not to have on her conscience the flight of this new client.

From his tiny lips, he whispers an unexpected request: "I want a voice," he says.

"I'll give you my poor daughter's "I say, smiling happily.

# WHO

Naturally, the first time I became pregnant, I was very nervous. I didn't know how things went, the phases of pregnancy and labor. So, where to start?

When I perceived that from all appearances I was not expected, I set about watching carefully, hour by hour, the way the operations unfolded. I understood very well that my will would not intervene.

My vigilance did not go uncompensated. The child was born normally but this must have been a miracle because at the time I was not mature enough to know how to determine what was important in the creation of a human being.

Since then, I have certainly changed. Confident in my experiment as soon as I have conceived, I let things take their course. At least during the long months my control is involuntary. I pay little attention to it except for insuring the quality of all the things that go into the body, properly speaking. I am proud to have, up to now, managed fairly well to bring off this secondary task.

On the other hand, everything starts for me at the end of gestation. The live being, finished inside, already functions with its animal instincts; I feel it. It could exist, when the time comes, without any intervention on my part But who will it be since I will not agree to give it a face, this attribute, this seal, this public space wherein is located, concentrated, displayed, all that drives the shadow of man?

The last minutes are terrible. Irresolute, weak, conscious of my responsibility as far as the pain goes, terrified and as a result losing all power of imagination, I look around: sometimes perched on peaks and crests here, or there, rolled along on relentless streams. And the days pass on the reddened face, deserted, so innocent that it claims nothing.

At full term, when I have no doubt that prevaricating will make me give birth to something: a pot, a wooden spoon, at best a doll, and suddenly grace comes to me. I find.

# THE ERASER

I.

THEY ALWAYS SAID OF ME: "SHE IS SELF-EFFACING"

"Self-effacing..." As a child, this word made me think of a portrait in pencil disappearing under the friction of an eraser. I imagined, under the rubber peelings, something faded like a very old photograph.

I was docile in my role of wary wall-flower. At parties when I was a girl, I was forced to attend with the intention of "civilizing" me, I remained in the background, silent. At formal gatherings and balls, I preferred to stand behind a pillar or on the threshold of a door. People greeted me for a time, then I was forgotten.

Undoubtedly I had stopped being seen because people, men and women, bumped into me and did not excuse themselves. Groups wanting to seclude themselves for private conversations came to stand near the place where I stood hidden without worrying about my presence. I heard nothing of what they said, nothing other than a battery of words that made me un-comfortable.

II.

It happened that one night returning from a party I noticed white stains on my body. Some resembled hands, others a piece of a hip, belly, or shoulder blade.

Later, I noticed that on returning from my walks, I brought back traces of different things. They were imprinted all over me, blurred images, fragments of people or harnesses, fixed in their tracks. In the beginning, it all disappeared the next day and then returned when next I went out. Which is no longer the case today. The marks are now cumulative.

Now, things in nature even amuse themselves in torturing me. The trunk of a tree, a bit of obscure cloud, the direction of the rain, they all remain inscribed on my skin. For the last few days, I see my skin in places turning from scratches to dust. I am growing thinner.

III.

"She is self-effacing..." they said. No...not yet, but certain they are trying to rub me out.

This evening, I said to myself it would be less humiliating to take action myself and in the most concrete manner.

Before going to bed, I took my child's eraser mockingly and, planted in front of my mirror, I began to pass it over my cheek. What a surprise to realize that this operation was so successful. My face is no longer symmetrical. A light void hollows out the right side in parallel rows like claw marks on moist plaster. My eye is worn, sealed, the eye of a corpse. In the same way a corner of my mouth will never again pull itself back.

It won't be long. Tomorrow I will continue my work, and each successive day, until finally I am totally annihilated and without help from anyone else.

* Images to accompany "Who" and "The Eraser" by GISÈLE PRASSINOS may be viewed in the article "Dead Metaphors of the Avant-Guard: the Case of Gisèle Prassinos", Miller, Margot, *Interdisciplinary Humanities*, University of Louisiana at Lafayette, Fall 2005, 22.2 (14-21).

# SHAD DANIEL MARSH

# FRAGMENT #8

If the rain thinks
that this is an emergency,
can we organize it
into something like speech?

...

Never a mountain wanted
over rain;
its formlessness is a
repetition            tho
of what no one is quite
sure.

...

Nothing can sleep like the rain,
whose irony is never
quite far behind.
Each drop an
erasure of what
comes before.

...

If the rain is an abstraction,
then each of its bodies
rise, perilously, black and
breathing.

...

The rain is a door
that opens and closes
like an eyelid straining
to watch,
against sleep,
its first opening.

# MARY BARRES RIGGS

# NIJINSKA AT WORK

Bronislava Nijinska was staging her ballet *Les Biches*,
which she had premiered in Monte Carlo
with Diaghilev's *Ballets Russes* in 1925.
In her seventies, she styled her fine grey hair under a white net.
Every day, she wore the same black polyester pants, green
and black batik print shirt,
and white knitted slippers with pompoms.
She shuffled around, demonstrated steps with her hands,
and whispered *"glissade, brise, jete, assemble."*
Her slanted eyes mothered me —
the raw sixteen year old learning to dance a vamp.
She taught me how to flaunt and flirt as the house party hostess,
how to play with my pearls,
how to take the deep *chasse*,
how to jazz the low-down drags,
how to improvise my *port de bras en ménage*
before I basked on the blue couch and drew the men in.
As I learned the "Rag Mazurka" in *Les Biches*,
I could smell her perfume — "Fame."

# PONTS DE COULEURS

"Man lives in two worlds...without a bridge between these two worlds {the logical and the intuitive}—...man has no guide for daily living. **COLOR IS THAT BRIDGE.**"

— Reuben Amber

## I. Black

I slide my hand over the arched back
of the ebony chair drinking *Schwarze Katz*.
The old witch scrying the obsidian ball
divines the red-haired flirt in the little black dress.
In *Shambhala Agartha*, I stand before my yoga teacher.
She has long black hair. The light shines from her eyes into mine.
Black stone of the Ka' aba at Mecca
Black Madonna, hidden one—
"She has labored in her brother's vineyards; her own she has not kept." (Cant: 1: 5-6).
Black Kali, Mother of *mantras*.
The Black Swan seduces the Prince.
Someone steals my onyx ring.

## II. Red

*Muladhara*, root chakra, foundation—I climb Jacob's ladder.
The dragon knows the pomegranate, the red thread, and the Rose of Sharon relate rituals.
Why does Mary Magdalene wear red robes?
I pen the little X.
The Firebird flaunts her magic feathers.
The flamenco dancer in the red dress kicks her flounce,
Throws a rose, flicks her fan. *Duende!*

## III. Orange

I stretch near the canna lilies spiring orange plumes.
The gypsy rose is dancing a *fandango*.
Orange zest enlightens my spice cake.
Eve's apple was an apricot!
Apricots are plentiful in Kashmir.
With my glass slippers, I step into the pumpkin carriage.
Amber, fossilized resin of coniferous trees,
we peer into a million years ago,
looking for mosquitoes and ferns.

## IV.Yellow

"Jewel of the Lotus," Gaia is alive—she breathes, she feels, she prays.
The Chinese Emperor wears yellow robes with dancing dragons.
Yellow stones, ruled by Mercury, are a solar storm piercing the earth's atmosphere.
The Citrine is a psychic stimulator like a lemon squirting a wake up call.
Summer is slicing the spiked top and rough skin off the pineapple.
Yellow diamonds fly my poem like a kite.

## V.Green

Heart chakra, Sophia
Peridot, malachite, and jade, lovely sisters
Four-leaf clover in the Emerald City of Oz
Green is the color of my fairy ancestors—Gille Sidhean and Melusine!
And don't forget de Vere! *Vero nil verlus*!
The Green Stag drinks from the Grail Chalice.
I stand beneath the green kudzu shower with bright purple flowers.
I savor a spoonful of key lime pie, watching seagulls on a Florida beach.

## VI.Blue

Throat chakra, blue dragon lines are the *nadir* of Mother earth.
The Blue Boar, family badge of the Archdruid
Our Lady of Lourdes wears a white dress and blue sash.
Blueberries, blue hydrangeas, bluebells—they even have blue roses now!
The "devil with the blue dress on" does break the rule,
except when she is dancing to "Moon River" in a quiet room.
The Blue Girl in *Les Biches* is chic—
pirouetting from *pointes* to *pointes*.

## VII.Indigo

*Ajna chakra*, third eye, color of the midnight sky.
Sapphires deepen my understanding.
I see things in their true colors.

## VIII.Purple

On the Pala Indian reservation, the Indians gather lepidolite, a mica rich in lithium.
At the Abbey of *Regina Laudis*, they grow lavender.
The Lilac Fairy waves her magic wand.
Nymphs weave a circle dance, celebrating the harvest of the grape.

"I am the vine, you are the branches." (John: 14)
"Come beloved, it is time.
Let us go together into the vineyard to see if the vines are in
bloom." (Cant: 7: 13)
Purple is the color of Lilith and her descendants — the Royal Elvin
Race.
I give my daughter a pair of amethyst earrings.

## IX. White

Crown chakra, the shaman carries quartz on his journey to the
World Tree.
Pearls are sacred to Isis, Venus, and Diana.
*Sylphides* wear them when they dance.
The moonstone is sacred to Selene.
I wear the white swan cloak of my ancestors.
I travel to the "Land of White Waters," to the center of *Shambhala*.
Angels sip champagne on coconut clouds, watching rays of light
intersect a waterfall leaping off the edge of a cliff.
The glare of wedding white blind me to the yes and no.
I slip my finger in the diamond ring.

## Notes:

The title, "Bridge of Colors," was inspired in part by Amber Reuben's
book *Color Therapy* (New York, 1983) and by many other books
concerning yoga, philosophy, and science. Nine is a sacred number
in many religions and philosophical traditions. The poem includes
both personal and esoteric references and highlights my love of
language, sound, dance, symbolism, and world mythology.

### Black

Line 3: *Schwartze Katz* is German for "black cat" and, in this
case, refers to a German wine of the same name.

6. Victoria LePage in her book, *Shambhala: The Fascinating Truth
   Behind the Myth of Shangri-la* (Wheaton Illinois, 1996) presents
   Shambhala as an enteric city. The hidden-valley legends
   belong to the tradition of "concealed treasures" or termas.
   Shambhala relates to a view of Mother Earth or Gaia as a
   living astral being with *chakras* (energy centers) and *nadis*
   (nerve channels) akin to those of the human body as elucidated
   in the science of ayuveda and yoga. Tibetans and other
   initiates believe that Shambhala is in touch with the light-
   world or subtle spiritual realm, an energy that is outside
   our concepts of space and time, but manifest in our terrestrial
   world as *kundalini shakti,* and in this form abides at the
   World Axis, the center of Shambhala. Shambhala is not
   allied to any religion or creed. The divine shaku has been

compared to the dark matter of the Universal Energy Field. The Axis Mundi is the uniting principle of the Cosmos. The shaman knows that kundalini is present in the energy body of the earth, and through ritual and trance, he seeks access to the World Tree and the pleromic state of potentiality. The true shaman receives initiation from the spirits of his ancestors. Some initiates suggest that the druids of Britain has access to the *Kalachakra*, the Doctrine of the Wheel of Time, whose teachings guide one to telepathic communion with Shambhala.

7. I had this vivid dream during the time I was studying yoga with Karin Stephan and Patricia Walden at the B.K.S. Iyengar Yoga Center of Cambridge.

9. Margaret Starbird, in *The Woman with the Alabaster Jar: Mary Magdalene and the Holy Grail* (Rochester, Vermont, 1993) extends the symbolic blackness of the bride in the canticles to the "Lost Bride," Mary Magdalene. Many shrines to the Black Madonna are scattered throughout Western Europe. Classical replicas of Isis and Artemis of Ephesus were usually black. Margaret Starbird and others are calling for a balance of the female and male principles.

11. Kali (Sanskrit: Kali) is a Hindu goddess with a complex history. Kali is the femine form of the Sanskrit word "kala" or "time." Kala also means black. Therefore, various translations of kali have been "She who devours time." "She who is the Mother of Time," and "She who is black time." Some devotees regard kali as the Mother of the Universe. Kali is the unmanifest pure energy, the Adi-shakti. The goddess kali should not be confused with the kali yoga of Hindu cosmology, as her name has an unrelated meaning. Kali is the mother of language and all mantras. A mantra is a mystical syllable or poem, usually in the Sanskrit language.

13. I worked as a ballet dancer in Hannover, West Germany in the early 1970s. We were not allowed to wear personal jewelry during the performance, so I left my onyx and gold ring on my dressing room table during the performance. When I returned, it was gone.

# Red

14. In *The Dream Legacy: Secret History of an Ancient Bloodline* (San Diego, CA 1985-2001), Nicholas de Vere, descendant of the Earl of Oxford, writes on the history of the Dragon Peoples, and the Fairy and Eleven Race, the Shining Ones, the Watches. He references his secret family archives and intuitive abilities. He describes the ritual symbolism of the pomegranate, the red thread, and the Rose of Sharon as they relate to the Kaula Varma Marg of Tantric Yoga, the Dragon Rite of Enthea or Starfire, and the ritual duties of the priestess of Isis or Hathor.

18. The little red X was a secret symbol of the heretical church, which stressed a balance of the masculine and feminine as the true path to enlightenment. See Margaret Starbird above and Harold Bayley's book, *The Lost Language of Symbolism* (Great Britain, 1912).

21. *Duende!* A Spanish word, often applied to the performing arts, conveying the emotion, passion, authenticity, and energy of a live performance.

## Green

44. *Veno nil verius* is the Latin motto of the Earls of Oxford, de Vere. It translates as, "There is nothing truer than truth." I am a descendant of the Earls of Oxford. Nicholas de Vere and others trace the ancestry of the Earls of Oxford to Gille Sidhean (pronounced Sheen), whose name means "Steward of the Fey." The Earls of Oxford bore the hereditary titles of Knight of the Swan, Oberon, and Lord of the Ring. They held the badge of the Archdruid, the Blue Boar and claimed descent from the Archdruid, Bran the Blessed.

## Blue

55. Bronislava Nijinska choreographed *Les Biches* to the music of Francis Poulenc with set designs by Marie Laurencin. The ballet premiered in 1925 in Monte Carlo with Diaghilev's *Ballets Russes*. The costume for the blue girl is a short blue velvet tunic.

## Purple

63. The Abbey of Regina Laudis is a monastery of contemplative Benedictine women living under the guidance of the Roman Catholic Church and following the rule of St. Benedict. I lived on the grounds of the Abbey in Bethlehem, Connecticut and I will always remember the lavender and Mother Benedict Duss. Lavender is reputed to be a favorite flower of the Blessed Virgin Mary; it represents purity, virtue, and cleanliness.

## White

74. In *Shambhala,* Victoria Le Page asserts that most mythologies of the World Tree have life-affirming images, whereas the Hebrew version subverts the meaning to instill fear, blame, guilt, and punishment. See pages 156-157.

75. The swan cloak represents the poetic and intuitive powers of the shaman/priestess as well as her role in sacred rituals of enlightenment.

## SUSAN V. CARLOS

# BAYOU CHURCHYARD

Tumbled cane slumps
tattered rows
to hollow swamp

where blackbirds brood
on racks of leafless limbs;
thin hope in mid-winter

lingers on five pale tombs,
whitewashed with
faint sunlight.

# DENNIS SALEH

# THE MASK OF NARCISSUS

The world is fescennine and vermillion
with dusk's lurid insistence

The chalice of the moon lifts
to the obvolute manner of the colors

wrappings round into night
relieved at last they are gone

It is not surprising to find one's self
lost at the skirt of evening fall

The moon concentrates one
like a mirror

But here is the myth of Narcissus
What he would not give to be himself

to slip into the mother-of-pearl
and become white a canvas

become less himself in
a painting of a mirror

The mirror is the mask
Narcissus fixes himself in

and turns round to the world
but do not ask him to sign it

He loves no one Not himself
Sleep searches the night

through in silence remedy
to his dreams but in vain

He stands before a great sea
which mutes sullenly

Echo at the far end of the water
says with the waves Narcissus

## BENJAMIN MORRIS

# ON THE INTERPRETATION OF WALLACE STEVENS

She called his thought a *line*,
and after playing a tape
of the wind hovering
over the lilacs,
closed the door and
left the room — and there,
in the dark, hearing
the murmur of angels
as they conversed upon
the beautiful and the still,
we slowly understood,
until one of us began
to cry, and others, to leave.

# KAYE VOIGT ABIKHALED

# KENYA

The sparkle in your eyes is happiness,
grateful acknowledgement of home again,
where the fortress watches sunsets blaze
into Lake Travis, where sisters wait and lilies bloom.

*We hear you've been to Kenya?*
and you answer, *Yes, tall palms, orchids and hibiscus
business is well, projects are on track.*
Steely twinkle, thin lipped smile

beard turned white hiding lines of worry
posture tight, holding your heart in,
cordial pats to shoulder blades. —
You've been to Kenya

neglecting to mention the tug at elbow,
sudden exits through hidden gates,
Mercedes side swiping mazes,
garbage, excrement, road kill, screams,

sprinting on foot through broken fence
lifting off before the door is latched
tree line skimming, ragtag mercenaries
wasting ammunition. Missions for a people

bent on lifting off your head.
*You've been to Kenya?* —
and you tell us
that nothing out of the ordinary happened.

# CAROL FRITH

# SHE IS SO BRAVE

Her skin blue as a Matisse cut out, she is a cold nude turning away from her interior. At this moment, no song agitates the indulgent turquoise space around her. Lace cap hydrangeas scribble messages on the blue air, seconds lost without a clue, a breeze of yellow fluttering on her left. She is familiar with the present tense, its lack of white space, its uncertain metric. *Zed*, she says, reencountering the yellow. She has come here to walk in the bright garden, to count the tropic birds, and there is no end to the convoluted path marked "odd" that she is walking down, the light around her rueful and bright. All Thursday she will stroll here, daylight shuddering the clematis, cockatiels swaying and shrieking, and no one to translate the flowers into Latin names—the birdcalls into tropical vernacular.

Every parrot is a magician. Eva told her that. She has long since shaped each of Eva's words into a shimmering stammer. A parrot startles the quiet dust, marginalia of swift green flashing from its flight feathers. There are flowers here brief as scented ink on bond paper. *Eva*, she remembers, pressing the letters into the flesh of her left palm, Eva disappearing into spider orchids and fern. Two tanagers, out of place among the macaws and parrots, squeak like tropicals.

She imagines closed space, that part of afternoon where the moon isn't yet, flowers spacing themselves outside of color, bird calls singular and precise. She will wait here for Eva, a book of light in her blue lap, the garden impressionistic—a bit more complex than she had imagined. The light changes, afternoon shaking the static from itself. *To be in a garden*. She attributes the infinitive to Eva. Switching tenses eludes her.

Flowers secure themselves everywhere—balance on her book. She has forgotten the birds, their cries vague now, their voices foaming. What happened to the azaleas, the rhododendron blooming outside of winter? Much of the flora here now is ground cover, plump yellow composite heads littering the floor of the garden.

Night is coming, concentric rings of lessening light dissolving illusion. She counts her angled breathing, whispers as the dark comes down. She's careful not to listen to the parrots, to distance herself from the flowers. Macaw after macaw floats away over the twilit garden. *Eva*, she says again, preserving her focus, an Escher moon swallowing one by one over the tropical patterns in her voice.

# MITCH COHEN

# THE FEAST OF HOLY INNOCENCE

The meal, we were told, would be glorious; each course brought tableside on the backs of bent and naked Africans. Under domes of gilded silver easily matching any of Europe's cathedrals in brilliance lay the smallest and rarest of creatures, slaughtered in their infancy and grilled to perfection; these, we understood to be delicacies. Wine flowed mercilessly and laughter, affected and glaring sharp, grew and leapt in the hall, resplendent and lit as it was by tallow and spermaceti candlelight, a thousand flickering points of light. The meat tasted well of death on my tongue, but I chewed on regardless, as did those on my either side, forcing our throats to swallow and partake in these riches.

When once the floorshow was long done, dancing girls clearing pancake from bruises behind the thick velvet boundary and hidden from our view, the maniacal ringleader uncapped and pissing in pain in a pot past the stones which slowly killed him, the pathetic clowns succumbing to their own brokenness and sweet, pungent, tobacco smoke rose to heaven from mouths and pipes and cigars as from censers, the lights came on and it was time, they said, for all of us to go.

Outside, in the biting cold, despite a thousand years of protocol, there was no one to bring around our cars, and flames just over the wall somewhere lit the night sky like pyres. I feared for my life. While no one in the group—standing in the unforgiving wind, carrying upon it the burning stench of flesh—was surprised, the sense of shock amongst us was palpable. How could it be, how in Heaven's name, we cried aloud to one another, how in the Name of God and Heaven and all that is Holy could this ever be?

# IAN WILLIAMS

# ETUDE IN E, OP.10, NO 3

—Frédéric Chopin, bar 46

The phone interrupts a scale.  A late
    night nailrun down the black keys
        because I happen to be passing

by.  The call is quick and quiet.
    I barely knew her.  I shake
        my head though no one is watching.

Then I go outside (too late, yes) and water
    the new mulberry and the grass seeds
        trying to sprout. *Lord she wasn't even 30.*

No one knew how long she was dead
    walking around the terminal
        of some disease waiting for her plane.

I might have caught it when she stopped
    matching her purse to her shoes.
        I might have caught it then, had I

been around, and not practicing
    the same bar of Chopin again and again
        (I eventually got it) the bar

when the whole etude crashes
    into shards, the reckless intervals, the
        hell with it

(last wish was to have her nails
    done) bar when the etude fails.
        That bar she frequented.

Have mercy.

# FRANKIE DRAYUS

# (DIGITAL) PICTURES AT AN EXHIBITION

*This life has been enhanced for anamorphic widescreen:*

Every culture has a Christ and I don't mean The Messiah. I mean every culture has a scapegoat we murder in public. Then we eat him. I have read Joseph Cambell and I am going to Hell. It is the flesh of revenge (love your neighbor) and the milk of human kindness (got any?) and if you covet this *capture,* have a trusted biographer (have 12): Matthew Mark Luke John Peter Paul & Mary: 2K + 2K= more *K* (scan): amber means sticky and thicken; it means years from now I'll hold you as you were: O sap of the earth: O emulsion & egg white (accentuate the positive) – if that photo doesn't look like me but it is me then – honey, it's *so* you. But I never talk like that. Never dress like this (lady in red) can't believe I'm doing this never drink this much (jutter j u t t e r ).

*These dishes in your sink are best viewed at 1.85:1.*

Cleanliness is next to *you were never here.* O acquisition and scan (some pot) (no pan): I want credit. More credit. A credit as large as the director's. A slower                    rolling

       credit – I want more of me in emulsion. More of my life in this ointment.

O Andy I will fuck your 15 minutes and birth an heir – an era: Pleistocene, Jurassic: *this* is how to (bleibe, reste) *shtay* – better to curse the dark (on record) (during Sweeps Week) than light a doomed candle in a room with no camera. How many *flicker flicker*? How many mm to amber? If I know a song of Africa – if wishes were horses – if Frankie and Johnny were lovers (were subject to gun control) – everyone gets what's coming to them, of course. The trick is how to be fabric and loom. Cat and cradle. Hollywood and Vine. Mussel and shell – "Kissing your scarred skin-boat..." (*Don't worry – we can fix that in post*) Merrily merrily merrily life *is* but a dream. But amber is every dreamer. Behold. Be *held.*

---

Notes

..........

Various and sundry

*"Kissing your scarred skin-boat..."* comes from a long poem by Michael Ondaatje called "Rock Bottom."


*Capture, acquisition, pan and scan* are film making terms and apply to digital as well as analogue.


*Jutter*: the shaking of the projector causing the film to jitter and shake when projected.

# DEREK POLLAND

# CONS (EQ)UENCE

Vine Street. Midnight. Streetlights.
Yellowing across. Sprung into it,

*[overlapping text, largely illegible]*

nothing else left for us to do.

There slips backward and kisses itself
In the other room, the baby nuzzles
the bottle close. Our street, morning

Old Hannah burning the back into

The bottle. How green enough. Limning
the edge. The broken edge. The lip

making of this poem nothing more

The gristle of these words, this poem

of found cash.                There was a sense

left behind. A stutter that was stuttering.
                                                   was stuttering.

              Is this poem enough?
Vine Street. The newness of the bottle—

The gristle of these words, this poem
which                                                     isolating
nothing                         for us itself. Every part kissed
                    disappears. Passing from the kissed.
In the other room, the baby nuzzles

this poem and make of it something
                                              Is this the poem?
These people. The remnant of a kiss

*[vertical marginal text, partly legible:]* begins to lighten — begins to brighten — Green glass. The horizon. — begins to

# NANCY DEVINE

# FEMININE PROTECTION

Small Rorschach of blood
on the crotch of my underwear, I wait
on the stoop of our cabin.
Oaks and birch shelter me;
sunlight sneaks past their leaves.
He delivers—this husband of mine,
someone who, like me, used to be just another stranger
wandering the planet—
tampons, pink, plastic-covered heads up
stringed stems down
in the vase of his left hand
this bouquet.

# CHRIS PASCO-PRANGER

# 11419-11506

| Form **1040** | Department of the Treasury—Internal Revenue Service **U.S. Individual Income Tax Return** 2004 | (99) | IRS Use Only—Do not write or staple in this space. | | |
|---|---|---|---|---|---|

For the year Jan. 1–Dec. 31, 2004, or other tax year beginning , 2004, ending , 20

OMB No. 1545-0074

**Label**
(See instructions on page 16.)
**Use the IRS label.** Otherwise, please print or type.

L A B E L

H E R E

Your first name and initial **CHRIS** Last name **PASCO-PRANGER 11419-**
Your social security number **11 ┊ 50 ┊6**

If a joint return, spouse's first name and initial **i. ITS: Controlling the Future::** Last name **so it's written on the back of a van:::**
Spouse's social security number **you ┊ mi ┊ss &**

Home address (number and street). If you have a P.O. box, see page 16. **and it's more true that--'swept along by every wind of teaching'-** Apt. no. **-control**

City, town or post office, state, and ZIP code. If you have a foreign address, see page 16. **resides in hands. You predict the swing's arc with your fingers;**

▲ **Important!** ▲
You **must** enter your SSN(s) above.

**Presidential Election Campaign**
(See page 16.)

Note. Checking "Yes" will not change your tax or reduce your refund.
Do you, or your spouse if filing a joint return, want $3 to go to this fund? . . . ▶

You: ☐ Yes ☑ No   Spouse: ☑ Yes ☐ No

**Filing Status**
Check only one box.

1 ☐ Single
2 ☐ Married filing jointly (even if only one had income)
3 ☐ Married filing separately. Enter spouse's SSN above and full name here. ▶
4 ☑ Head of household (with qualifying person). (See page 17.) If the qualifying person is a child but not your dependent, enter this child's name here. ▶ **and**
5 ☐ Qualifying widow(er) with dependent child (see page 17)

**Exemptions**

6a ☐ Yourself. If someone can claim you as a dependent, do **not** check box 6a . . . .
b ☑ Spouse . . . . . . . . . . . . . . . . . . .
c Dependents:

| (1) First name    Last name | (2) Dependent's social security number | (3) Dependent's relationship to you | (4)☑ if qualifying child for child tax credit (see page 18) |
|---|---|---|---|
| **ii. the Home De(s)pot** | **exp ┊ ec ┊ts** | **burnt** | ☐ |
| **offerings, the residue** | **of ┊ a ┊ fail** | **ed fuse, this** | ☐ |
| **tyrannical dream.** | **Sta ┊ li ┊n ex** | **pected the** | ☐ |
| **deputies to applaud after he** | **spo ┊ ke ┊unti** | **l he sat.** | ☐ |

Boxes checked on 6a and 6b **land**
No. of children on 6c who:
• lived with you **in a**
• did not live with you due to divorce or separation (see page 18) **net**
Dependents on 6c not entered above
Add numbers on lines above ▶

If more than four dependents, see page 18.

d Total number of exemptions claimed

**Income**

Attach Form(s) W-2 here. Also attach Forms W-2G and 1099-R if tax was withheld.

If you did not get a W-2, see page 19.

Enclose, but do not attach, any payment. Also, please use Form 1040-V.

| | | | | |
|---|---|---|---|---|
| 7 | Wages, salaries, tips, etc. Attach Form(s) W-2 | 7 | Once, after an | epi |
| 8a | Taxable interest. Attach Schedule B if required | 8a | c speech, he | did |
| b | Tax-exempt interest. Do not include on line 8a  **8b  n't sit for hou ┊ rs.** | | | |
| 9a | Ordinary dividends. Attach Schedule B if required | 9a | The clapping | ran |
| b | Qualified dividends (see page 20)  **9b  g down like ┊ ste** | | | |
| 10 | Taxable refunds, credits, or offsets of state and local income taxes (see page 20) | 10 | el on steel. | Som |
| 11 | Alimony received | 11 | e in attendan | ce |
| 12 | Business income or (loss). Attach Schedule C or C-EZ | 12 | fainted at the | eff |
| 13 | Capital gain or (loss). Attach Schedule D if required. If not required, check here ▶ ☐ | 13 | ort, others w | ent |
| 14 | Other gains or (losses). Attach Form 4797 | 14 | mad. | On |
| 15a | IRA distributions  **15a  a recording ┊ of** b Taxable amount (see page 22) | 15b | the event, the | app |
| 16a | Pensions and annuities  **16a  lause takes u ┊ p a** b Taxable amount (see page 22) | 16b | n entire side | of |
| 17 | Rental real estate, royalties, partnerships, S corporations, trusts, etc. Attach Schedule E | 17 | a vinyl lp. | The |
| 18 | Farm income or (loss). Attach Schedule F | 18 | clapping com | es |
| 19 | Unemployment compensation | 19 | to sound like | art |
| 20a | Social security benefits  **20a  illery fire in a ┊ Sib** b Taxable amount (see page 24) | 20b | erian night: | |
| 21 | Other income. List type and amount (see page 24) **explosions frozen in ice like** | 21 | wayward ma | mm |
| 22 | Add the amounts in the far right column for lines 7 through 21. This is your **total income** ▶ | 22 | oths. | |

**Adjusted Gross Income**

| | | | | |
|---|---|---|---|---|
| 23 | Educator expenses (see page 26) | 23 | iii. You were | bor |
| 24 | Certain business expenses of reservists, performing artists, and fee-basis government officials. Attach Form 2106 or 2106-EZ | 24 | n to volcanoe | s |
| 25 | IRA deduction (see page 26) | 25 | tectonic | all |
| 26 | Student loan interest deduction (see page 28) | 26 | y. Out the wi | ndo |
| 27 | Tuition and fees deduction (see page 29) | 27 | w I could see | Mt. |
| 28 | Health savings account deduction. Attach Form 8889 | 28 | Ranier; in the | roo |
| 29 | Moving expenses. Attach Form 3903 | 29 | m the great h | eav |
| 30 | One-half of self-employment tax. Attach Schedule SE | 30 | es of your m | am |
| 31 | Self-employed health insurance deduction (see page 30) | 31 | a's body. Th | e f |
| 32 | Self-employed SEP, SIMPLE, and qualified plans | 32 | lesh around h | er |
| 33 | Penalty on early withdrawal of savings | 33 | vagina swelle | d o |
| 34a | Alimony paid  b Recipient's SSN ▶ **ut ┊ wi ┊th t** | 34a | he pressure | of |
| 35 | Add lines 23 through 34a | 35 | your emergin | g s |
| 36 | Subtract line 35 from line 22. This is your **adjusted gross income** ▶ | 36 | kull like the | gr |

For Disclosure, Privacy Act, and Paperwork Reduction Act Notice, see page 75. Cat. No. 11320B Form **1040** (2004)

**36**

## Tax and Credits

| | 37 | Amount from line 36 (adjusted gross income) . . . . . . . . | | | 37 | | |
|---|---|---|---|---|---|---|---|
| | 38a | Check { ☐ **You** were born before January 2, 1940, ☑ Blind. } Total boxes | | | | | |
| | | if: { ☐ **Spouse** was born before January 2, 1940, ☑ Blind. } checked ▶ 38a | **o** | | | | |

**Standard Deduction for—**

| | b | If your spouse itemizes on a separate return or you were a dual-status alien, see page 31 and check here ▶ 38b ☐ | | | | | |
|---|---|---|---|---|---|---|---|
| • People who checked any box on line 38a or 38b **or** who can be claimed as a dependent, see page 31. | 39 | **Itemized deductions** (from Schedule A) or your **standard deduction** (see left margin) . | | | 39 | und around | a v |
| | 40 | Subtract line 39 from line 37 . . . . . . . . . . . . . . . | | | 40 | olcano would | sw |
| | 41 | If line 37 is $107,025 or less, multiply $3,100 by the total number of exemptions claimed on line 6d. If line 37 is over $107,025, see the worksheet on page 33 . . . . . . . | | | 41 | ell with mag | ma. |
| • All others: | 42 | **Taxable income.** Subtract line 41 from line 40. If line 41 is more than line 40, enter -0- . | | | 42 | I was terrified | at |
| Single or Married filing separately, $4,850 | 43 | **Tax** (see page 33). Check if any tax is from: **a** ☐ Form(s) 8814 **b** ☑ Form 4972 . . . | | | 43 | the time | of |
| | 44 | **Alternative minimum tax** (see page 35). Attach Form 6251 . . . . . . . . | | | 44 | lahars-- | whe |
| Married filing jointly or Qualifying widow(er), $9,700 | 45 | Add lines 43 and 44 . . . . . . . . . . . . . . . . ▶ | | | 45 | n ice melts o | |
| | 46 | Foreign tax credit. Attach Form 1116 if required . . . . | 46 | ff of a volcan | ic | | |
| | 47 | Credit for child and dependent care expenses. Attach Form 2441 | 47 | glacier, the w | ate | | |
| Head of household, $7,150 | 48 | Credit for the elderly or the disabled. Attach Schedule R . . | 48 | r rushes dow | nsl | | |
| | 49 | Education credits. Attach Form 8863 . . . . . . . | 49 | ope picking u | p s | | |
| | 50 | Retirement savings contributions credit. Attach Form 8880 . . | 50 | ediments of a | ll | | |
| | 51 | Child tax credit (see page 37) . . . . . . . . | 51 | sorts, becom | ing | | |
| | 52 | Adoption credit. Attach Form 8839 . . . . . . | 52 | a wall of slurr | y t | | |
| | 53 | Credits from: **a** ☑ Form 8396 **b** ☐ Form 8859 . . | 53 | hat moves as | fas | | |
| | 54 | Other credits. Check applicable box(es): **a** ☐ Form 3800 **b** ☐ Form 8801 **c** ☑ Specify t as a speedin | 54 | g drunk drive | r. | | |
| | 55 | Add lines 46 through 54. These are your **total credits** . . . . . . . . | | | 55 | It buries all i | n i |
| | 56 | Subtract line 55 from line 45. If line 55 is more than line 45, enter -0- . . . . . . ▶ | | | 56 | ts cement. I r | ead |

## Other Taxes

| | 57 | Self-employment tax. Attach Schedule SE . . . . . . . . . | | | 57 | In the paper t | hat |
|---|---|---|---|---|---|---|---|
| | 58 | Social security and Medicare tax on tip income not reported to employer. Attach Form 4137 | | | 58 | there was a | mid |
| | 59 | Additional tax on IRAs, other qualified retirement plans, etc. Attach Form 5329 if required . | | | 59 | dle school on | an |
| | 60 | Advance earned income credit payments from Form(s) W-2 . . . . . . . | | | 60 | old lahar flow | in |
| | 61 | Household employment taxes. Attach Schedule H . . . . . . . . | | | 61 | Puyallup. If | |
| | 62 | Add lines 56 through 61. This is your **total tax** . . . . . . . . . ▶ | | | 62 | another one | flo |

## Payments

| If you have a qualifying child, attach Schedule EIC. | 63 | Federal income tax withheld from Forms W-2 and 1099 . . | 63 | wed from Rai | nie | | |
|---|---|---|---|---|---|---|---|
| | 64 | 2004 estimated tax payments and amount applied from 2003 return | 64 | r, the school | wo | | |
| | 65a | **Earned income credit (EIC)** . . . . . . | 65a | uld be buried | un | | |
| | b | Nontaxable combat pay election ▶ | 65b | der 40 feet of | cra | | |
| | 66 | Excess social security and tier 1 RRTA tax withheld (see page 54) | 66 | p in 20 mins. | It' | | |
| | 67 | Additional child tax credit. Attach Form 8812 . . . . . | 67 | s about 20 mi | ns. | | |
| | 68 | Amount paid with request for extension to file (see page 54) | 68 | from the sch | ool | | |
| | 69 | Other payments from: **a** ☑ Form 2439 **b** ☐ Form 4136 **c** ☐ Form 8885 | 69 | to high groun | d. | | |
| | 70 | Add lines 63, 64, 65a, and 66 through 69. These are your **total payments** . . . . ▶ | | | 70 | The fat kids | wo |

## Refund

| Direct deposit? See page 54 and fill in 72b, 72c, and 72d. | 71 | If line 70 is more than line 62, subtract line 62 from line 70. This is the amount you **overpaid** | | | 71 | uldn't make it | |
|---|---|---|---|---|---|---|---|
| | 72a | Amount of line 71 you want **refunded to you** . . . . . . . . . . ▶ | | | 72a | | . |
| | b | Routing number | i | v . a f r i e | ▶ **c** Type: ☐ Checking ☑ Savings | | |
| | d | Account number | n d o n c e t o l d m e t h a t o | | | | |
| | 73 | Amount of line 71 you want **applied to your 2005 estimated tax** ▶ | 73 | ur name soun | ds | | |

## Amount You Owe

| | 74 | **Amount you owe.** Subtract line 70 from line 62. For details on how to pay, see page 55 ▶ | | | 74 | like a trapeze | act |
|---|---|---|---|---|---|---|---|
| | 75 | Estimated tax penalty (see page 55) . . . . . . . . | 75 | I listen in the | dar | | |

## Third Party Designee

Do you want to allow another person to discuss this return with the IRS (see page 56)? ☐ **Yes.** Complete the following. ☐ **No**

Designee's name ▶ k under canvas for the sound　Phone no. ▶ ( of ) applause: it ri　Personal identification number (PIN) ▶ | n | g | s | t | h |

## Sign Here

Under penalties of perjury, I declare that I have examined this return and accompanying schedules and statements, and to the best of my knowledge and belief, they are true, correct, and complete. Declaration of preparer (other than taxpayer) is based on all information of which preparer has any knowledge.

Joint return? See page 17.

Keep a copy for your records.

| Your signature | Date | Your occupation rough the tent and says don' | Daytime phone number ( ) t ever sit down S |
|---|---|---|---|
| Spouse's signature. If a joint return, **both** must sign. | Date | Spouse's occupation adie, your occupation is set. | |

## Paid Preparer's Use Only

| Preparer's signature ▶ | Date | Check if self-employed ☐ | Preparer's SSN or PTIN You swing i |
|---|---|---|---|
| Firm's name (or yours if self-employed), address, and ZIP code | ▶ n the klieg lights, it smells of elephants, popcorn. Kids clap like rain as you float on tyrant air. | EIN Phone no. ( ) | |

Form **1040** (2004)

**37**

# MAURICE OLIVER
## IMAGES. SKINNED. EATABLE.

-A phone ringing into shampoo lather.

-Time needed to devolve apparatus.

-The amount of paperwork needed to get a rental car.

-Difference between the Grand Canal & Grand Central.

-A bar code on a box of dominoes.

-A garden show of slow bloomers.

-Trying to tell an aspen from an oak.

-A textbook intended to accompany Grievances 101.

-The razor that slipped in the shower.

-Cactus in a petting zoo at high noon.

-Nocturnal animal caught in a TV screen's blare.

-Vodka that speaks with a Finnish.

-The privilege of pleading temporary insanity.

-Quite a bit of acting for a ham.

# JEAN-MARK SENS

# SNAIL

Curious lodger, the snail that beats the hare. All contained in the shape of a circular stair that ends to the navel of its shell. A question to the philosopher, the far, the near do not exist for this sluggish creature that carries its shelter on its back. Where does it go? What does it convey twisting its antennas like hands of Vishnu? Anchorite of the garden salad, lover of the curly cabbage head that slowly finds the way to its heart, sure it is wiser than a King Lear Tom the Fool would say. Mostly solitary, it takes walks only in family after the passing of the rain, a strange interloper that lost the sea for its frontier sluicing its wet belly over ground leaving a shiny, dry-salt path. An odd inhabitant of its shell though rubbery, claimed edible stuffed with of a lot of garlic and butter, replenished with parsley greener than any emerald leaf that it ever devoured and endeavored.

# JOHN HARVEY

## LOBSTER EN CHEMISE

In my history of gastronomy, I sift the moon through the finest horsehair. I hold a saucepan just so; slowly add sugar, lavender and dark trees. Nobody pays attention to this. Goodnight to chicken livers and knowing where you are. Goodnight to believing slices of mutton slightly flattened and fried in butter can fill the time of a man whose wife has left him. Once it was a matter of flies: blue-green

abdomen on a water jug, a cobalt blue plate collecting blue specks in my grandmother's kitchen—adder and fern bluing into ash. I sit in a restaurant and watch light settle across spotless white linens, champagne buckets, my father's fingers spooning cold pheasant soup into an ache patient and hungry.

The menu promises Burgundian snails, racks of lamb, and fine copper pots. My father lists everything he's buried, while the sun staggers around, knocking over plates of stewed rabbit. He cries that his brother died alone. I've never been to his damn grave, my father shouts as I cart him back home. Below the rooms IU rent on La Estrella, a small boy sells horn-handled knives and fish half-buried in ice.

I tell him that Rouen duckling is smothered not bled and this gives the sky its unique flavor. He's not impressed, says his aunt who is pregnant, belly out to here, whispers love masquerades as a napkin folded, pressed to lips, and passed in a clockwise direction until everyone's wiped their mouth, then it's opened.

# RATS

The child looks into the rat's eyes. Try to eat it, the rat thinks. Light gathers its day like mouse-holed entries in an old Larousse: pilaf of larks, larks with risotto. Take a plump little boy, sprinkle him with salt, then thrust him into your mouth and chew hard. A face like sugar mixed with a spoonful of wine, small cake for a wedding night.

The rat loves a good murder mystery. *They had not even buttoned up her blouse, and some white underclothing was poking out of her mourning dress.* Delicious. Season with pepper. Saute with olive oil and garlic. The rat rolls rat-eyes into crawl spaces behind its skull.

Squatters carry folds of Tyrian purple. They finger liver-red crayolas into gas-heater nozzles, smear tar across cupboards, rub saliva and bittersweet into a low, sad love song. The rat believes a child's open mouth can find truffles in marrow-soft grass.

Shopping bags ride in the sky's juice. A young girl's glass eye rolls into weeds as neighborhood boys strip blouse and skirt, play in the half-light of an abandoned warehouse.

Time to separate out the bones, the rat smiles.

# F.J. BERGMANN

# COMPANION TO THE GUIDE TO THE NORTON READER

Norton Reader, though experienced enough in the more civilized English forests, was understandably reluctant to venture into our savage wastes without a trusty pathfinder—the uncultured lout in whose concubinage I languished. I had come from significantly further west, with a native gift for language and communication. Despite the squalling infant at my breast, I managed to recover memories of landmarks that would beckon us to our objective, furnishing a personal report of people, place—and the lay of the land.

I had not foreseen how Norton's magnificent breath and splendid, upright stance would dwarf my common-law spouse's less-robust frame. The comparative considerations were not lost on me. Despite our education disparities, our minds were one, and my heart was a moon that swelled with wordless longing, metaphorically speaking. I began dwelling upon analytical considerations, and, in rhetorical mode, made circumlocutous suggestions as to the unreliability of firearms, the judicious introduction of vipers into sleeping-blankets, the variety of herbs and fungi at hand; but the critical resolution was ultimately provided by a perturbed grizzly bear—coincidentally, also a mother.

"Norty," I murmur, "Oh, Norty!"

Reader, I....

# RULING CLASS

*This test has been scientifically designed to assess your reasoning skills. Write the answers in block capitals, using Roman numerals only. No extra pencils, bathroom trips, or religious practices are allowed.*

I.    If two trains leave their respective stations at the same time, one traveling at 50 mph westbound and one traveling at 80 mph eastbound, at what point will their trajectories intersect, killing 117, injuring 84?

      Why do we use the term injuring instead of wounding or maiming?

      Which engine crew was smoking marijuana? Defend your reasoning. (25 points)

II.   The best-laid plans of men and angels are not implemented. Why? Discuss. (20 points)

III.  A virtual (but extremely convincing) fire breaks out immediately beneath your loge at the Opera. How crowded should the theatre be (specify density with regard to structural volume, discounting catwalks, restrooms and backstage passages, will suffice) before shouting "Fire!" will do more harm than good?

      If the exit does not manifest in 25 seconds or less, it is not meant for you.     You could take the long way through the smoke, but why bother? Elucidate or adumbrate, according to your personal philosophical beliefs. (15 points)

IV.  Country A, whose population comprises 21.8% of the planetary total, requires 87% of a particular commodity to support the practices of 3.1% of its citizens. Country B, with 34% of the planet's population, would like to have 50% of this commodity, which it intends to distribute equally among its citizens. Country C, where the commodity is produced, has a famine and 0.7% of the population. 75% of its citizens have access to firearms and / or explosives. Produce a regressive rationale for prior and subsequent events that does not conflict with the doctrine of whatever agency from which you intend to someday request funding. (25 points)

Total possible points: 85

*The remaining 15 points are reserved in the form of a voluntary gratuity furnished to your hard-working instructor. Points will be deducted for defective personal ideologies. Any use of emotions will automatically result in a grade of F. When you are finished, crawl beneath your desk, put your head between your knees, and wait for further instructions.*

# MARK TERRILL

## LA RUE FEROU

Paris streets underfoot,
cleaving to history,
someone else's memory
burned into my own.

Remaining alive
by staying attentive
to the immanence
of daily life.

Man Ray's old studio
in the rue Ferou
now occupied by
someone named Roswitha,

or so it now says,
on the tiny nameplate
next to the brass doorknob,
polished and gleaming,

time's inexpiable code
cracking, fracturing into
the vowels and consonants
of the present moment.

# RYAN FOX

## THERE SHOULD BE GODS

who demand no tribute to be mentioned
by name in the sort of vagrant conversation
one has with oneself before sleep on a winter night
when even the smaller animals are denned
and waiting is over, when the work is done
and the water tastes exactly as it should.

# ERIC RAANAN FISCHMAN

# METHOD POEM

the incandescent pagans like parking meters
with red elbows blinking and the noon
in your cortex / so what if the sun
is a thousand fireplaces / so what if
light is not light except to the dark / the
earth is full of steam, your white eyes
sizzle to the touch / and we are rendered
thoughtless as clouds or Zeus's pockets
when they have been emptied of quarters

# G. DAVID SCHWARTZ

# GERTRUDE STEIN AND INRICO BAR BETT BEN BASSTED LOCATE A THOUGHT ABOUT A POEM BY WHITMAN

(Things denoting the end, or beginning of a statement Lady I am thinking about what queries you raised Period (Things denoting the end, or beginning of a statement

(Things denoting the end, or beginning of a statement Yes Comma kind sir Comma and what do you happen to think Question Mark (Things denoting the end, or beginning of a statement

(Things denoting the end, or the beginning of a statement Well Comma Lady Comma I think the rabbit was a bit innocuous Period (Things denoting the end, or beginning of a statement

(Things denoting the end, or beginning of a statement Well Comma that too but mostly obnoxious! (Things denoting the end, or beginning of a statement

(Things denoting the end, or the beginning of a statement Well Comma kind sir Comma what do you suggest we do about it Question Marx (Things denoting the end, or beginning of a statement

(Things denoting the end, or the beginning of a statement Ahhh Comma I am sorry but we can do nothing Period

(Things denoting the end, or beginning of a statement No Question Mark And why is that Question Mark (Things denoting the end, or the beginning of a statement

(Things denoting the end, or beginning of a statement Ahhh Comma because we have a bit of something else to get done Period (Things denoting the end, or beginning of a statement

(Things denoting the end, or beginning of a statement Ahhh Comma me lady Comma and what is that Question Mark Question Mark

(Things denoting the end, or beginning of a statement Kind sir Comma it is to find another kingdom in which we may live in quite unnatural peace Period (Things denoting the end, or beginning of a statement

(Things denoting the end, or beginning of a statement Ahhh Comma your sweet person Comma I do agree Period (Things denoting the end, or beginning of a statement

(Things denoting the end, or beginning of a statement Well Comma then Comma off Period Off we go! (Things denoting the end, or beginning of a statement

# ARTHUR E. HOWELLS II

## AT CEFALU IN SICILY

The Scarlet Woman[1] milks an axe handle at her hip
She crushes a cross with her heel and kisses Nybra's[2] ass
William Perry[3], the Bilson Boy, says he saw it,
The square: sator, arepo, tenet, opera, rotas[4]
And was given thumbscrews and Vaseline to cleanse her
Miriam the Jewess[5] (half sister to Moses)
Also hiding her nudity beneath a red cloak
Spread in a dusty street in Cefalu[6] and smiled
As a fylfot[7]–wheeled chariot ran over her body
She is served by a crucified toad (her dead god)
As Haxon's[8] reel-end flicks against a bright bare bulb
And the golden ropes of the sky hang everything

---

[1] Wife of Aleister Crowley
[2] A devil who rules over sex in hell
[3] Testified falsely for the church against women accused of witchcraft
[4] The oldest and most significant magic square
[5] Famous sorceress
[6] Site of the Abbey of Thelema, the home of the Scarlet Woman and Crowley
[7] Swastika, as used in the Black Mass
[8] Silent satirical film dealing with the practices of witchcraft

# ISIS MOURNING OSIRIS

The serpent is an animal that can see
the whole of the universe in a man's eye

...

He was born tongue-tied
The four hairs on his chest formed a swastika

...

Dogs lift their snouts to the air of the charnel house

...

Isis weeps for her husband and brother
as the sun's master, judge of the dead
is reduced to ash

...

Rows of granite sink and rise
shaded and un-shaded by the oaks
and a shifting sun

...

Afraid of being stabbed by the Italian
he had the barber shave his face and head

# RENZO LLORENTE

# AFTERTHOUGHTS, AND OTHER IMPROPRIETIES

1.

As we walk down any city street we are perfectly aware that all
the people around us are, *underneath* their silence, carrying on
endless soliloquies; yet we are hardly moved, on these grounds
alone, to question their mental health. Were we to walk down
the same street and find the same people carrying on their soliloquies
*aloud*—exteriorizing their monologues, so to speak—we would
regard each and every one of them as hopelessly deranged. To
think that the *differentia* between sanity and madness should be a
matter of *decibels*!

2.

It is little wonder that people are so ready to grant that so-and-
so—usually a writer, thinker, political activist or the like—is the
"conscience of our time": it relives them of the responsibility of
having a conscience of their own.

3.

To have unclear thoughts is to mumble *in silence*.

4.

It is often said that a nun, in assuming her vocation, becomes
"the wife of the Lord": Does that not make her the social climber
par excellent? How else to regard one who *marries into the family
of the Almighty*?

5.

It's hard to say whether God overreacted to the mischief he discovered
in the Garden of Eden, but surely there can be no doubt that as an
act of *collective punishment* his achievement remains unsurpassed.
For Yahweh's response to one man's lapse was nothing less than...*the
condemnation of an entire species*!

6.

As Cioran rightly observes, "It takes an enormous humility to
die. The strange thing is that everyone turns out to have it!"
(*Anathemas and Admirations*). It is equally true, of course, that
the dead manage, miraculously, to *maintain* this humility. This is
surely not the least of their virtues, and undoubtedly the one
that most endears them to the living.

7.

A friend was told that a woman whom he had worked with for several summers had killed herself. When he later encountered the woman in a department store, he was, needless to say, stunned. Fortunately, he was still able to collect himself and bite his lip before uttering the obvious, yet *peculiarly unspeakable,* phrase: *"But I thought you'd committed suicide!"*

8.

How explain the inability to give *oneself* the benefit of the doubt? Whence this compulsion to *anticipate one's detractors*?

9.

Gargantuan malls, immense supermarkets, department stores that mock any pretension to "human scale"—the commercial institutions that surround us and define the contemporary landscape long ago renounced all efforts to appear "familiar," or to minimize their impersonal feel: *massification* is no longer burdened with a bad conscience.

10.

It may seem remarkable that those who have *the least time*—the old, the elderly—have *the most patience,* but this is no doubt the true hallmark of their wisdom: having grasped that it makes no difference in the long run whether they do one thing or another, they are indifferent to the delays that prove such a torment for the rest of us...

11.

*Prayer as megalomania*: The believer starts a conversation with himself—and tells us that his words are addressed to God!

12.

"Never miss a chance to have sex or appear on television" (Gore Vidal). Sage counsel, to be sure, but in some sense the maxim implicit in "amateur pornography" plainly goes one better, as the genre is nothing if not a celebration of having sex and appearing on television *at one and the same time.*

13.

We perform a tedious job that requires sustained concentration: *we squander consciousness.*

14.

Whence the condemnation of *loitering*? Why this aversion to what is, after all, the definitive metaphor for "the human condition" ("to remain in an area for no obvious reason" (Merriam-Webster's))?

15.

The chief virtue of moving about foreign lands? The *mundane* never loses its novelty. (Edward Dahlberg: "When one realizes that his life is worthless he either commits suicide or travels" (*Reasons of the Heart*)).

16.

Theology is the *pious* form of sophistry.

17.

The "occupational hazards" of astronomy: To be reminded, day in and day out, of one's utterly negligible *stature*, to see one's complete significance "experimentally confirmed" on a regular basis! (Astronomy — the *abysmal* science.)

18.

The problem with any *failure* is that it tends to summon up so many of one's previous failures; worse of all, it tends to *substantiate* them. (Depression, Cioran remarks, produces a similar phenomenon: "By virtue of depression, we recall those misdeeds we buried in the depths of our memory. Depression exhumes our shame").

19.

"Liquor and Christianity" are, according to Nietzsche, "the European narcotics" (*The Gay Science*). Two World Wars, genocides, inquisitions, countless imperialist depredations...: One shudders to think what the Old World might have accomplished *without* sedation.

20.

When others find us in their act of reproaching ourselves for some minor failing or misdeed, they often assure us, by way of consolation, "Your being too hard on yourself." That is to say: "Don't be as hard on yourself as you would be on someone else."

21.

Suicide is an extreme act, to be sure; not least of all because its utter *superfluousness*. Suicide — the "gratuitous act" par excellent.

22.

Barthes once suggested (in *Lover's Discourse*) that to *know* someone is to "know his desire." What, then, does it mean to be someone's *friend*? Is it not both to know that person's desire and, in a certain sense, to *share it*?

23.

Satisfaction at the death of another — the supreme expression of *Schadenfroth*.

**54**

24.

"T.V. does the same thing to human relations that frozen food does to real food" (Norman Mailer). No doubt this is the reason that at certain moments there seems to be something positively sacrilegious about turning on the television.

25.

To think that one can point to no *hobby* other than relentless self-dissection!

# ANDREW SHELLEY

# CRASH COURSE

Sleek steel-grey vehicle speeding through sunlight to where the road peters out on the beach in slap-dash cement clinging to brick-ends, mudpuddles of sandpitted tentwater and blocks of conglomerate struck to torn-up scabs of surfacing. Jump-cut jolt-started from handscrawled signs, instance is simple tense, place made over entirely to time. Kickstarted from handscratched marks, houses are outposts of distance. Eaten under wheels stripped of all history, that progress without aftermath, where you were is where you are now set back along the axis. A single timeless virgin present processed pointlessly forwards, translating future to now exactly blanking past as expelled detritus. From absolutely inside, all without look like escaped killers, all seem nude, moving as smudges at the margins of the screen, blurring to merge beyond this sealed place whose soundless murder is self-defence against all silence. Touchbutton windows effortlessly glide shut without seam to subtract self as distinct from its backdrop, extract viewer from its sights, relieve seer of thing seen. So vision is magnified to vista eyelessly. Incommunicably itself everywhere and exemplifies self without residu, each of which is not there. Gradually nearing, fleetingly proposed as instant only to be wiped out at the moment they come close. Scanned, excised from sight in the matchless light of the shatterproof shield, it's the landscape shifts to your static demand for action. Self breathes here so bulletproof against any but its own noiseless feedback you can be shot dead for sounding or forgiven for screaming if disturbed from such sleepless cinematic dreams. Track is fodder to that bodytight mindspot from which all time and place have been sucked clean out through the seething vents' stitchless pleats. At night, senseless metal shells circulate around each other in a frictionless element of dancing lights, where all contact is collision. Beams streak streamlined through the aquamarine dark. They meld to perpetual noon at midnight. In the abattoir on the outskirts of town, electric lights shine till dawn.

Shot out of a tunnel, out of a frame-gap, out of night as space of mere lack, a masking, a blocking, a blind-slat, a bridge-strut, a salt-brick, thin wall between vast windows that engulf the whole view. Class concept slices through a landscape of samples in infinitely receding series, each extinguished as soon as it is instantiated, whole lush world leased to us by the sovereign sign itself unsignifiable. Moves forward by continually touching and spurning the ground it touches. All designates that which once itself described. World destroyed once it is abolished to the imagination. Fleshtight eyedot, vacuum-wrapped, styles itself into a zone of pure forms to hover over the faceless tarmac on a cushion of smooth space, purchase of its rubber base on the surface repressed beyond texture or grain, but still needing to move on. Smoothed out from the centre, everything ripples to rough and sharply grazed enough at the edges to shred hands that claw through the incinerating steel mesh seeking water. One touch deletes what is already not there, matchstick shack shimmers down, fragile membrane of the egg's yolk pricked by a flame-carry on blinding to denial until it includes everything and seamlessly there's nothing but itself to omit. Gunshot report like a thundercrack. From crouched foetuswise between frames of the arrested fast-forward film your dark double slowly uncoils and rises up to snipe at fingers. Someone shouts at the rain-blurred fringes. Someone unspins at an eye's edge. Pixel by pixel the lightscene reforms in gradually accruing drops on the screen that the burst and every contour is obeyed. Travelling into a horizon of louring haze, rain oil-drumming on metal through wet-bleared windows, forced through the gorge where the radio goes dead. Rain cross-hatching the roadscape, grey-black rubbing of zinc or lead, waterlogged rain-heavy ink-dark blue-black sky, dimension drowned-out. Inside you hear the waterecho of receiver whiplashing the signal live back on the streaming screen but somehow holding to it in motorway stormrain. You home your engine in fast lane to the transmitting tower shifting in grey rainmists but still lighthousing you to a point amid millions of gale-dashed points of cross-slit slash-silver which rimshoot off the chrome and whip-crack the signal to keep the godsped wheels from skidding. A bird's wet throat chirping rebirth as it drinks from a milkbottle full of rainwater on the step, arrived overnight as the guests of the frost's breath.

## BULL

We were not deep enough into the eye of night to hide from heaven, nor far enough away from the fallen city to forget the heat. My heart was a hand opening and closing inside me. Throbbed within me like a small trapped bird that wanted to break free of its shell and fly away. Frozen in ice, deep underground, stood transfixed and rake-thin body of the ancient naked warrior, dull thunder crumbling over him, groans of the gradually melting ice surrounding him, flesh slowly peeling off his wirey body. Eyes half-closed, palms turned a little outwards, head slightly downturned and to one side. Lips pursed and semi-smiling, as if about to speak, or having just spoken, pausing to think, breathe and consider an instant what this quiet was, what this darkness whispered. Fleeing peoples flooded a plain. I was far enough into the heart of the light to forget the night. I was deep enough into the heat of the sun to heal the hurt.

It was not evening, it was morning and night and my heart pounded like footsteps to heaven, beat like a fist on a door that wanted to open and let God in. Life's knocks were just raps on the heart's trapdoor that strained to open and allow light and love in. Dealing with your pain had the meaning of nursing the world's, for at root both were the same. The lowest bore the burden of the earth, and in so bearing it, kept it afloat, hovering in the air. The sun

was so harsh it was like sunbathing in the searing fire of a nuclear
bomb going off very slowly. Tanning ourselves in the world's last
instant protracted endlessly. Reclining languorously on our black
leather plinths. Then it was not morning or night but some timeless
suburb of time suspended between summer and autumn, and the
stars were glittering as brutally as suicide, when the fat bull's
head, followed by its great bulking body, crashed to the floor of a
small sun-dusty circular arena of heat-hardned sand, floodlit and
paved with marble grave-slabs whose inscriptions were polished
to illegible scratches. The bull's big yellow eye gaped like full
moon at floodtide. Blood-stained ribbons, tied to the stakes in its
streaming back, quivered; its liquor ran hot and thick into the
chisel-cut ducts that spelt the charm's design, the talisman's name,
the figure that designated all cardinal points as collapsed into
this one central cradle, this single pivotal axis, this core of carmine
ink into which the women dipped the sleeves and hems of their
muslin clothes, ripped them off and wrapped the blood-soaked
strips tight around their bodies bruised blue and rubbed sore-red
by men and labour. The hard ground, cold as a corpse's scalp and
bald, began to yield to tree and field and cracks in the frost-scoured
plain filled with seed. But a rind of bitterness sicklied over sweetness,
an obese death-maggot squatted inside plenty and people cried
and died when they tongue its acrid spite inside the covenant-
crop the bull had fathered. From the cracked tree of tillage that
grew where the bull's slack blood spilt, fly-blown dead men hung
like plump fruit. So I bore the bull's body like a black sun on my
back far away to a deserted stony place where I set it down and
sat and wept until my tears were a dark dank lake from which the
stars drank their shine. And from their faint reflected light I
laboured to fabricated a crystal-clear palace of systems built of
ice-facets turning perfectly in the air suspended propelled by its
self-sustaining need to appreciate each of its flawlessly cut edges
in turn forever. I smashed it at once and smelled inside how the
fanged bloody yawning maw of its vaunted devouring emptiness
was filled with the reek of this slaughtered bull's rotting corpse;
saw how each of its faultless aspects was one segment of a fly's
eye gorging on that carcass.

It was not night, it was morning and evening and death-crazed
priests darted around in bullmasks and little white fluttering frocks
earnestly and assiduously officially slaughtering each other with
sacrificial handaxes according to holy tenet, wise maxim and modern
instance, having denied that the bull's wide round dead eye coined
each of their images in exact reverse. Danced ringaround the hallowed
empty well of shallow gunk holding aloft their handless bloodied
armstumps gleefully. Their white morrismen's dresses with ornately
embroidered hems wafting in the breeze like butterflies' wings
merrily. They'd severed with a schoolboy's blunted penknife the
artery that was their lifeline to the mortal animal and were startled
when their veins began to jig around them like so many snakes
walking upright spitting acid fire. Some myth of connectedness
was a miraculously extrapolated into a religion of severance, celebrated
by cutting the writs of human relatedness, such that we were so
divided from each other we forgot what we were derived from at
root and had to maul open each other's torsos to find again the
lost child of the truth we'd refuted curled up inside out projections

and denials at their core drenched in gore as if the brat had never been born. The altar table was spread for the death-feast and over its sickening virgin-white cloth I spattered blood of the bull as if the colour red webnt unproved by mother's dewfall menses. Which obstinately refused to be redeemed as wine. I nailed the bull to a cross in Christ's stead but they screamed blasphemy and seized the cross and set it back in place propping wide the very abyss between earth and heaven into which huge shoals of tiny white naked chirking souls poured ceaselessly. So I stripped off my skin and sloughed off my flesh in big slobbering fistfuls and stepped out all bull all sleek wet and streaming. I saw through myself. I bent my head and prepared to charge while at my back the dull thunder of a thousand stamping hooves was heard.

## CLEAN

The difference is I can't rest without their manifold othernesses that were nibbling me all over so that I was giggling constantly at the edges. Entering sleep. I shrivel like something too hot for it. I'm ammonic; bleached so clean. I need water.

I was more interested with them nesting in me, those bytes of the context, those topoi, those binding-sites networking me all over to time, place and instance; pinpointing me to something broader than me impossible to define. I'm all border, or none now they're not constantly eating the death that exfoliates from me moment by moment and in return feeding me their subtle antitypes. In siphoned pinprick mouthfuls converting I to not I and vice versa. Wanting scroungers, I've no burthen to drop and begin to float up and away in every direction, introducing myself without difficulty and noticing my too polished smell like scrubbed pink pork. An awful quiet has settled deep into me or is it that I hear my sterile body continuously throbbing to itself for something to contradict it. Fleeced down to the raw for riches' sake, there's nothing but the reek of me, stink of cleansed, clariform. I torture in others this my own stench, skinning, at safe distance, theirs from them. And paring in to the layer that's hospitable only to scabs, poached tender, I exude claw around that sweetest part. In the mirrored shopping palaces, the boiled clothes of the highly finished people itch

I'm homeless without them lodging in me – those public creatures instinct with my privatest spots, those circuits of translation, those bits of home spoiling into the street. I run around constantly on call while something in me crouches on the steps like a lost dog, getting bewildered, because it can't get savage enough. Turning vicious, because it can't carry on being totally confused. Without that map of sites, those plotted loci, my house is changing into an office, a space I merely hide from belonging nowhere. My earnings arrive in the form of damages for injury, ransom for kidnap, court costs, the price on my head I'm hunted for. When cars overtake I shudder as if I'd been crushed and in the centre, where it's harder for pushers to get the hell out of the way, I feel like elbowing them in the gutter, in self-defence. The sharper my suit, the more thuggish I seem, the more naked I appear, shabbily fleshed. Shorn of that common pelt that keeps people at arm's reach, they veer clear, or latch on and sink their private lancets with ease, probing my liquid wells to strike it rich and lucky. Without those basics to background me, those breeders of the margins, there's nothing to distinguish me from others similarly so blindingly distinct you have to shut your eyes and try to envisage them- coffles, with bare feet in black shoes. What's left of the world's all one to me. I call this globally conscious: globs of individuals floating in some hypothetical community in cyberspace bound together solely by the fact that each of them reflects the total universe entirely.

But the more uniquely shined am I, the more officiously do I pick on the slightest divergence from the line. Enzymatic, my fat exacts its fractions from everything it craves that's openly given to it. For whatever I receive is only what I have scrapped and beaten you for. I'm free only in so far as someone has to pay for me, clean of all attachment. And there's nothing I don't have to kill for dearly buying into a whole that's not there as soon as I've chipped a way into it. I grow so prime, food can properly be charged with my greed for it, air with my need to breathe it and where would the earth be if it wasn't under my tramping feet? I climb so high up the crooked, crippled steeple I fall back flattened backwards screaming back to basic but come down on these so hard they shatter to pieces under the impact..., and I'm left with nothing but staring at my empty hands for bad luck.

Scoured with professional agents, those nodes leap off and start to pester. Down the road they turn into lost objects of my youth on sale in op-shops. They kip on public benches during lunchbreak, or squat on doorsteps and nag me for things until I shiver. I hunger for them to the pitch of my very hatred for them, my dreams of those tites being censored as they waft me their undulating antennae

Without them to scratch, I gouge deeper and deeper, trying to find the warmth I left on the surface, into the still patient body of my parasite, my mite, that I loathe the more I gorge on, mouthtube pulsing, too louse to be a predator, too predator to care whether I knife what I live in. Feeding on your areas of decay, depositing more as my detritus. I tremble with the sex-sense that wants to pierce you with a multitudinous spore and hang on for dear life, nose-down, needling inwards with my legs kicking in the air above pathetically resembling feelers

I want to get under your skin and lodge and lay there a tiny horde with very small vicious crab-claws scissor-guarding my permanently open mouth-like structure, which devours everything, from which nothing issues forth

I want to cling on to your pubis in colorful colonies of darkness by indelible pads that look like egg-sacs at the end of my sensing

**60**

creepers. Burst, I want my guts to crack unforgettably on your fingernails and launch an immediate scamper of fresh young runnelling all over your corps

I want to cling onto hairs of your moistest places and spawn-spew a brood that will overrun and conquer you till you collapse, riddled, to dust like a ship of empire buried in an avalanche of black shit

Clean as a war criminal, as a city rebuilt from ashes, as a sexfilm set,I lay in wait, as ready to kill as to cower, itching for you with my bleeding feelers scrabbling at the too smooth plane, while everything I touch I cut myself on and everything that flays me I yearn to feel

## JIHAD

cough/lap up your luncheon and launch it on the floor of a mop-top slop-shop drop your load in a dirty lock-up dry docked ditched (dead) in the drunk-thinktank dunked down on a dinner-date in a dirt-dump {in a driving-ditch} in the chip-shop's stocks

{fancy a spam javelin spankin' a meat-torpedo injectin' up the trolly-dolly's gary glitter?} who's the daddy who's the patsy drop your pants and do your fancy party dance around a prayer-mat jump-jilt jerk-start your twitching innards to the disco-drill dancin' and waltzin' your slop-top mop-head on a broomstick to your breast as a darlin' dreary ridin' it horsewise to the fuck-truck in the shag-alley and back again then down with the drearies in the darkroom to brush up your stuffed staffed in the dungheap's muck in with the lads how you're going to beat the heat black and blue and wallop the black man's mug all the colours of your favorite cricket clique's whites waving on a ragged flagstaff as a national brand flown at half-mast on the hangman's ghoulish gallows followed by an equal and opposite act of addition of army-approved surrogate supply-prosthetics in the wrong order then we're surprised the patient thrashes about madly unable to stand or even crawl to us on his (plastic spastic) knees the length of the corridor (to his welcome to) his billycan of slops for suppah

tear yourself to shreds of the other crowd's footie shirts with your clenched teeth and call that damage the sporting strip of your very own clan seething in utter silence blessed are the brats dressed in the garish gear of our sacred soccer team hallowed family of one you belong to the more savagely in that human socius has gone filtering the mess through the pores of its thin yet sturdy skin in a form we could begin to tackle and hack

butcher the boogey gore the golem into four as if to prove the indisputable veracity of nature's universal and ineluctable law of quartering blessing our sacrificial knives as those of the natural order for enchaining our suspects and flaying them into the true and better shape of us is only right and proper drop bombs on them followed by food parcels as if to confuse them into surrender not a good sport a straight bender of a fair darkie if you're ruled out beyond the lines beyond the lines beyond the traces of the tracks' strick edges set flush against the cliffface of electrified wire fencing where the voices are locked in and unlistened to or tormented into saying things agreeable with the lullabies the blubberbyes we whisper ourselves to sleep with the call that privilged knowledge of God's law vouchsafed to us in particular as his especial agentds bristling with nipple-electrodes, high voltage supercharged apark-buzzing {electro-shock} cattle-prods and iron pincers heated glowing-red in the fires of our zeal that our demon-lust to possess objects of consumption and belive in nothing but money and rank greed should be the only sane, set and sanctified was the tighter we apply our instruments of torture in times of store-wars to the vulnerable moist niches of our enemies, trying to make them confess themselvers as really ourselves in disguise, (black sack off their heads and uncle sam or Johnny bulldog would emerge alive and advertising fried chicken with a smile for all the family) –the harder we hammer the wedges into the rack to crack the legbones the louder the trapped words we can't hush scream down our fairytales the close-speaking we censor and project into the heads of anyone poorer in weapons and things than us, but richer in spirit, pates bowed in due reverence to us or for the axe of our denials

how would you like it if the Asians raided an English church looking for evidence of the British Empire the black man being forbad doesn't make everything white cracking down on the 'outside' doesn't reinforce the walls of our shelters made of shit and spit outlawing the darkness doesn't make our hairdos blonder abolishing the black in a blinding flash just makes things go darker later no house till we kill 'without' no day until we whiten the night no warmth until we've declared freezing illegal no food until hunger's been proscribed (not at home until we've abolished the whole world outside our windows)

no clean air unless breathing's been made compulsory and poison gas relegated to the Arab States no sight until all the blind have been provided with a pair of free prescription spectacles no response until all wear sunglasses to shield their priceless vision from bombblasts no sleep until the insomnia of reason breeding monsters been properly treated or all the dossers dressed up in business business-suits and dunked down to jobs in front of computer-screams raid the mosque looking for terrorism in a sacred space in a shipload of sugar bound for the shopsin the west which is the best how would you feel or think if they invaded an Anglican church looking for American warheads burgle the bedsite searching for machine-guns under the sheets in bed with the fundamentalist priest fire off nuclear missles into outer space trying to take over nothingness colonize the void for how can anything exist of anything's nothing/ white circle of the world must be blackened ion Dracula-man presenting breakfast TV angles a vampiric eyebrow at the oddie plugging the eco-milk why doesn't he turn into smoke in the morning light?

why wasn't he coffined at daybreak?  how can I rise if I can't
kick away the shoulders I stand on?

## ENTIFADA

billpost the black world white/wish-wash it clean with supreme
fistions blank the blooming buzzin world with pictionary play-
cards lift up your wobbly advert-boards to sound you frightened
answer yes or no or bang it out on your little toy-soldier's drum
issued free by the company at the office party with sheery and
paper hats when the jerk unveils the wizened figure of the raise
dashed off in black makerpen squiggles on a whitened (wimpy)
wiperboard flexing loose in its gilt plastic frame the bolus of
the bonus is always the same as last year's pathetic perk staying
exactly the same by regular increments of precise similarity
blue celeste of poesie holds up a sign/placards raised aloft to
vote for the victor time all laid out in a circle of waged hours/
arms crossed over your chest to delete you cheerfully jigged up
and downloading hands with those posted on either side of you
like thieves at the crucifixtion ashbrand fingers charred from
tamping down and stubbing out your smoldering cigar-cinders
· in the opening of any too open-ended eye/too-rounded mouth
high-powered thugs in suites and mercs fast-track office drop-
outs gambling for a square meal a fair deal with a book of food
vouchers dud scripts flame that tries to pluck itself from its
wick with bud-snuffing blackened fingers want to snip the roots
that feeds us fire and ichor not proximity to the water but your
station on dry land saturated foundations dissolving in sand

value-banks depleted grip us in fists of sweat to swat us against
the whitewashed cellar wall in a splat of crushed limbs splayed
(cruciform) at odd angles like stopped clock-hands pointing to
some lost aspect of 24-hour digital daylight saving time/smashed
up grabbed down twisted tight to off/clinched shut/panic selling
our selves out stroking the barcodes the backs of our heads/
shaved bald down to the identity pin singed & tinged into the
flesh with a steaming stamp of ratification/whisper the hairs
erect child's coral-ear buzzed with the hot-breath of whispered
curses sizzling imprecations that nest within and hatch as demon
baby bats bombafrding our heads for pickings swear-vow the
innocent silence down it scares us then we disbourse and diffuse
according to the digits logged deep into our logic-boards sunk
down into our soft bodies by red-hot tattoo-needles to prick
out and point up the price and penance of the tenet we've transgressed
swag bagged up and offloaded, text-bricks built to a sloping
block, a dammed bank, laughed off and tagged as branded/trussed
with fusewires at their necks stamp on each other to frank us as
valid/{etched to a flat-rate}

beaten-up, we're roughed as current/scuffed as marked shopsoiled
{face like a smashed mirror} down to the millgrist, swaggering
blank frank knows best bills sent back unpaid to Britsoc sender
as price on our heads we're hunted for being alive become drystuffs
used goods and no wild wet ones, staggeringly hand round the
severed head wrapped in a brown-paper parcel trussed with
ropes blood leaks through the tight-pressing cords, costed as
(running) current when the tune plonked out on the pub piano
pauses you've got to unwrap it important bonds sliced or cashed
out /knocked flat in the race for standing, the crush to crawl/

bowled upright in the dash to sit still high-powered crims in mercs and suits fast-track office delinquents dicing for a square meal a fair deal with a book of food coupons defunct shopping lists flame that tries to pick itself from its wick with bud-expunging charred-black fingertips want stow snip the roots that feeds us fire and ichor and a thimbleful of listless liquor to wet your wishful whistle

don't vomit in the begging-bowl (totals mount us)  whitewash the pink world blue/wish-wash it clean with ultimate fictions feed the fruit-machine the bent spent penny of want and wank the handle of work and wait for it to disgorge less than you put in as what you've won gilded milk tokens it's minted as your winnings/yearnings you've earned as your worth scrubbed-red sweet-scented flesh tendered as illegal cost off our heads and our hats would go with them flat caps off to the toffs and our skullrugs would stick in them/doffed to con speed-track office drop-outs corporate-crooks high-powered octane-fuelled jet-propelled salesstaff in workfleets of suits and mercs professionally defrauding everyone expertly/ stuffing their false coffers with crowns minted from our dreaming eyelight gaming for a fair meal a square deal with a book of betting slips blank receipts salary-tag around our necks like a greek's cross on a gold chain ripped off quickly bounty we hunt each other for/price on our pates we threaten each other with death for stun-gun at your temple you babble fluently for your life, man you're priceless rifle-butt down your throat you gag on about bullets and given a smack in the mouth you get lippy

girl in a black leather catsuit with a pink machine gun no-one gets to fuck punch is bludgeoning the judies to the truer and better shape of themselves sho in the head shop all you friends to the gaffers/the over-magnates all's brightly-lit serenity in the all-night hypermarket fulfilled desire that casts no shadows/eyes like shattered windshields you ain't nobody till someone smashes your convex face hollow opening your lergs spins the axes that plot us as/ as fixed exactly in two dimensions between x and y yanked sideways to a elongated line {where}  you've brought on as a breeder of dead metal striking a deal between dull matter and any sense of identity porno itemsd that kill desire not satisfy it thing-sickness, commodity-stardom, glamour of artifact-celebrity addicted to the self promised by purchase/present as orgasm as {blunt} no point of exchange product of sale that vanishes to dross immediately it is touched and you're more down than before with a self that is a mere object to itself become like a town-centre eaten away at core by commerce you have to buy into to blockbroker any belief or feeling you belong to yourself or a community called Engsoc.

so eggs sit left

# JASON TANDON

# DINING PARTNER OF CANNIBALS

The vines straighten themselves
There's no one to swing and scream
and wake the apes that batter dolls' heads
to find out what's inside
The toy maker in a dress too small
takes a carriage ride through black widows
A bunk bed in the way of an icy stream
where a pheasant has drowned in a gloved hand
A slug crawls from its belly
into the governor's cobblestone courtyard
Rotisserie gargoyles grimace
The bread is hard as knees
The chef's brass pot boils bed frames
Wine pours like smashed stained glass
Cigarette flambé with a thin slice of Gouda
A Republic of garlic relying on trade winds
to whet the appetite

# GEORGE MOORE

## CIRCLE SPLIT

Some will say they were waiting for this, the deadend of all directions, the mouth devoid of any human contact, the uncolored propagation of those universes which cannot be found or centered. Of course, they will be a little in error, just a bit, for the involvement with words does not preclude an eye for the outside; a box is no more an end in direction than is a word or its punctuation. This about evolution, how in six days the language was ruined, and it took another species really to sort out the simple difference. Go ahead and mention this anywhere, like down at the corner store you talk about incessantly, and you'll see how people can map old highways in

their heads without a pen or
when the trees have fallen
single cry. Now there's a
in an unobstructed past to
one world and into another,
the last that it would be as
up into dolls and strung out
be replaced by a static in
one perfect note. So much

even decent paper,
for centuries without a
possibility somewhere
lift ourselves out of
so far removed from
if all creation were cut
along the stage, only to
the air, and a sense of
depends on that stupid

chicken, and yet what does it mean to depend? Is not there an idea here? Little different it seems to some than pulping the environment for foul papers and quartos. But now we've come around again, or over the edge, and nothing really fits. Have you noticed how limits are a different kind of freedom, and have their own inherent dimensions? That's enough--well that and a little room, no doors or windows--and anything can be made to look preconceived. Like a child, in the old days, or the horses coming to a fence when you pass along the road, or the fires and all that lovely power in the equipment, standing still waiting, prepared for the first yellowish light, but uncertain at last whether to pump or manage, or just let it grow.

Oh God, how in
the world did this happen? Now
there's absolutely no chance of finding our
way anywhere, if we can't see straight to dump the
old bugbears. Of course, some like the comfort of sight-
lessness, while pledges still complain that without some sense
of order there would be mere amorphia. But then look closely at a
distant object out of your particular space and tell me that doesn't fit.
If it matters it does so for whatever reasons can be found out there, not
in some apt concept of what ecclesiarches augured was the big picture, all
of it, with a voice that rocks the television screen, even when doing so they
too would die. What sense does nothing make, after all? Oh, yes, perhaps a
good deal. But then, everyone does, or they pretend to, and the silence is

almost stentorian. So you build your own, or borrow one from the last great
set of masters, arms as big as elk thighs, heads as solid as the nucleus of a X
on an old map, and it works like anything else you wind, for a time, and in
perfect harmony with the lesser mechanical failures. Once, before these
worlds began to close in, people trusted that, the time that would glow
yellow, not blue, not because of some gramarye, but simply for the
future in it. Now things have come back around like a theater
with all the groundlings found in a hand-held device. Just the
facts, nothing lasts long enough to fall through anymore.
When you can see again, dream of that same space
with your eyes open, next to the night's vast
engines, or divide it into parts, before
& aft, bow and trunk. Now
crack it open.

After you said that, I was reminded of the dog who carried a wounded child from the snowy battlefield without so much as crunching a bone, and carried her all the way to shelter, although it was not a human refuge, of course, but a cave deep in the hills. Some thought it was about love, but the story was told by an old man who had lost his daughter in an air raid sometime in the previous war, and had come to believe that animals remember the way to safety based on imprinting through successive generations. The dog he had was, at least in his own mind, kin to the Saint Bernard that crossed that battlefield with the howitzers going off left and right and the biplanes diving like insects on the flesh of the bloodied field. He was wrong, of course, or not so much wrong as deluded. It was in his head, both the dog's genealogy and the fact of the daughter. He was never married. He'd had a dog but never a daughter, and somehow he'd transposed the two and now thought that the war was a way of reuniting the dead. Of course, his real concern was how he might be remembered, and so the story. But stories, he realized, are only shells into which we put the messy mechanisms of our own tenuous desires and failures. And also the one thing that means something. After that, he refused to clarify anything for me. Others at different times asked him for a description, an age, the way movement was a grace descending on us like light rain rather than a machine's treaded menacing across broken ground. And he would talk about the open field, the way the animal thought nothing of itself—as if it could have thought otherwise, we said—and made a beeline straight for the wounded child. It was only an afterthought that made it all tragedy and not real. The battle was between two groups of children you see. It was not part of the larger war but a consequence of that war. They were from different provinces and fought over the food drops. The blond children, of course, won. Then the dog had to be sacrificed or everyone would have starved. His voice often broke when he recalled that sad fact, yet his story was never complete without it.

# BARBARA FREEMAN
# ST. URSULA'S MIRROR

Fires that cannot be kept from slipping

Fire that screams

"Fire" in an empty theatre

A thin fire has thirteen colors

Fire does not only work in wood

The thirteenth month has no color

Cannot be subtracted

From a body consumed by fire

Wills bequeath black lightning

Sirens sing

Across slippages that cannot be

# CLIFFORD PAUL FETTERS

## FAKE FISH

But is he real or a fish
of wood, carved and painted silver?
He floats but cannot swim.
He sees a secret through dizzy
water but cannot dive to it.
Lying flat on the sea top
he looks like something that he's not.

# VALERY BRUSOV

# FIFTY YEARS

*(translated by Vera Arti)*

Fifty years–
fifty landmarks;
fifty years —
fifty ladders;

A slow rise
to the top;
rise in sight
of gossiping hundreds.

Straight or crooked
ladders jumped,
circles multiplied
under wind or weight.

Narrow distances
suddenly widened,
prospects of mountains
lowered, revived.

Where am I? — how high? —
half a century — as the foundation;
sedge of hollow bogs —
like velvet.

Where's here? — glades,
drunk on silence?
Even planes
can't reach them.

Fifty years —
fifty landmarks;
fifty years —
fifty eruptions.

Every day is a step —
and the minutes quake —
my thoughts and labor —
year by year.

Height...
　　Silence...
　　　　Stars-revelation...
　　　　　But I know —

Day by day
　　space will grow
　　　　and there is
　　　　　another prospect!

My footprint is small!
　　　I don't want to know
　　　　　the weight of years!
　　　　　　wind, you are not welcomed!

I want my way
　　to reach the large rocks,
　　　　before I dash,
　　　　　　tossed aside!

　Fifty years—
　　　fifty landmarks;
　　　　　fifty years—
　　　　　　fifty ladders. . .

　　　(Just one more time!
　　　　raise up!
　　　　　and let them gossip
　　　　　　at the bottom!)

# LEIGH PHILLIPS

# FAG HAG

The saccharine sweeties, the drenching honeys, the ever palatable primetime novelty that sucks you; the standard straw, the smell of warm Gucci and preening Prada. *Strike a pose, there's nothing to it;* he is a ball of lisping light that exfoliates a tired world. He is a cat. An idea that comes while driving at sunset. Beauty aides in the erasure of a volatile past. You are his pet, pissed off as an electric cold blanket. Coked up as lines of lust, choked up as burning bronchioles and flagging fallopian tubes. Travel safely. Without heat, and almost your boy, pacify your night away in the eye comes a sign seen for "almost heterosexuality," a quaint little comfort just on the outskirts of "I'd marry you if I were straight." All gassed up, you hope because you're dumb. You keep creeping back. This net is the only worth jumping at. Your watch has his affairs unfold with the curdled obsession of a jilted housewife until everything becomes sick like this town with binoculars. Myopic, you force your vision in, seeing a secret notion that he'll decide you're worth all the Viagra, seeing him slump off his barstool, tear his stockings and break a heel while crashing down dreams on Broadway and you're strung out on the periphery. *Face it sweetie, there is no innocent eye. Time isn't the only thing that flies. Why don't you find someone? I'm not going to change. You'll always be our—Homo-Goddess—why?* Seeing him in love again, seeing him win. See yourself age, mistrusting more men. Test waters with the effeminate, short of being women, saved women, safe men and others will follow where it's shallow. Instead a life passes. You feel little and lacking flavor, king of bony, without glitter. Always had a special savor for dry cornflakes and their magnified crackles, the burnt toast of a solitary breakfast. Go. Into the looking glass go sight seeing the self as a tattered, chaste forty and realize what was taken thirty years ago and how you feel with it gone. Starts at twenty, this love as an apprentice. A life spent squandered awkwardly in trunks of trappings, hating your sex, without mirrors.

# JUDITH STRASSER
# ON THE PATH TO BONNYRIGG

*September 13, 2001*

Rosehips big as crabapples
Blackberries verging on wine

Brown-and-yellow snails
pin-striped, spiral domed

Purple thistles, salmon poppies
The last of the fireweed

Kenneled mastiffs howling
behind the razor wire

Scrawled graffiti


**PROD's + PAPE'S**

**SCOTS WE ARE**

**ALL**


**THE DAVID McPHERSON HATE CLUB**

YU KILLED KENY U BITCH

Black horned slugs, enormous
A pensioner walking his dog

# PETER SPECTER
## TWIXT

Twixt (1)

I walk below the lunar ticks counting
on the multi-surface aspect aspic
lake which like a monitor rash hertz ice.

Twixt (2)

What do writers know but about writing
which no one in their right mind wants to hear
(only those in their write-mind want to here).
I count them useful as accountants
(though I'm one too, I take us to account).
we want to give everything we've got but
are often out of contexts.

# ZACHARY BUSH

# PARTICULARS

## KINGS COUNTY, NEW YORK

**FILE NO:** 83-2552 **IMMEDIATE CAUSE OF DEATH:** Death by Drowning

**AUTOPSY:**___ YES ____ NO(1) **DUE TO:** Questionable Circumstances

**EXTERNAL ONLY:** ___ YES ___ NO (2) **DUE TO:** N/A

**BY:** Jim Hemmingway, MD

**MANNER OF DEATH:** Drowning

**DECEDENT:** Zachary C. Bush **AGE/RACE/SEX:** 27/W/M **MARITAL STATUS:** M

**ADDRESS:** 6892 Courtland Street, Brooklyn, NY 11230-5203 **D.O.B.** 8-29-83

**DATE OF INJURY:** 9-1-2010 **TIME:** 1315
**HOW INJURED:** Bathtub Drowning

**INJURY AT WORK:** N **PLACE OF INJURY:** Residence/Place of Death

**DATE & TIME FD:** Last Week **LAST SEEN ALIVE:**

**DATE & TIME OF DEATH:** 9-1-2010 1315

**PLACE OF DEATH:** Home Address

**CONDITION OF PREMISES:** Home Drowning
**RIGOR:**____ **LIVOR:**_____ **TEMP:**_____

**HOSPITAL CHART #**_____ **GUN TYPE** _____
**SCENE VISITED:** YES **TIME:** 1500

**DATE** 9-1-2010

Jim Hemmingway, MD

## PARTICULARS SURROUNDING DEATH

**FILE:** 83-2552 **PAGE No.** 1/15

**SEE ATTACHED SHEETS FOR "PARTICULARS SURROUNDING DEATH"**

# DANA STAMPS II

## NON-LOGOS

*for Jacques Derrida*

on-glide onion cui-bono
no-account noumenon add-on
onlooker nocturno phono
noir nourrission bonbon
onomatopeya (k) volcano
noxios nonillion eon
onomastic (N) kimono
no-load notation log-on
one nomino soprano
not noumenon icon

ontology  on  domino
nol-pros  noon  come-on
onslaught  no  romano

nonaria nonfiction tampon
onerous norteamericano jalapeno
no-frills nonagon dead-on
only (O) piano
note nonpossession frission
oneiric (w) steno
noble notation axon
onanism nono mono
no-fault nonunion put-upon
on-site ondulatcion pro-bono

## DANA STAMPS II
## LES DEMOISELLES D'AVIGNON

Come on, give Posterity a Peak!

It never felt Real anyway––drum colors.

Doubt can be heroic: the process.

Though, *un*damn*it*, nobody cared enough

to interfere. Africa. Jungle Trix.

Picasso's use: a plunder. White


art in black face. The eye. *Have it*.


A canvas, not a coloring book, duh, d-dut

dut-dut- duh, duh, *duh* . . .

You entertain me well, Ol' Square Crow.

But the female crotch doesn't

have teeth, scared*i*pants. "Grassy-ass,"

that's cubist for Fuck you. mODern aRt.

       m     a     s     k     s,

m

               (pee-pee)        s,

     a          .

                    k

# DAN STRYK
# WALKING IN A DOGLESS WORLD?
*(On the Rarity of Perfection)*


My wife leaps backward, clutching me, as again my teeth gnash down, near splintering. Fierce black Lab we've nicknamed "Snipe" (play of wit from a safer place) barrels by us, snapping close, wheezing amid snarls. Unchained again, brute reaper of

his master's boundless trust. She loves him and, once more, she sets us straight, eyes upturned, her bathrobe barely fast—as he mauls the earth that could be us, then leaps back to his porch, *her* pet: "Big fake. He'll never bite."

But our walk's gone.

We never tell her this—nor the other owners of chained feists that bark like crazed machines on our approach. Or leap along, to dog our heels, when loose. But smile, tell them it's okay. Can't control all facets of this doggy life, ourselves. Press forward, arm around my wife, feign a gay wave back. Continue with the walk we'd planned, somehow each time forgetting *this*, to ease distracted minds in scenic fall. Swept colors of those lovely yards, that symphony of yellow, red, the softer trills of grey and brown, throb in our skulls like raging blood and howls.

# WEBS

Everywhere by August, woven swiftly between door jambs, beaten down: each time        we mar their perfect symmetry—that sunlike burst of conical rays— with philistines' blind heaviness, when banging in and out. Yet boldly, they stretch *glistening again* the following dawn.

Remindful at this time, each year, of our bullyish existence in a world in which, unthink-ingly, we bungle, crush, or eat. But cannot, for all of Myth's "Dominion," quell or totally control. Every year the same—reminded, in this season, of the glut of our necessity. That which we too often *must forget* …

And yet … the question looms again. Are they treacherous to us, or *we* to *them*? Each year the question looms the same, woven over doors and under desks, or blazing sunlit in warm woods….

*

I remember now—walking a woodland path I love (the same path through each season,        all year round, to sluff the hectic world and make me calm)—the *sudden shock*. Thin antler

of a "web-stick" waved before me, long forgotten, drooping from my hand, I'd felt the prick    of the micrathena—arrow-shaped and dangling above my brow, like a miniscule black kite. When, deep in thought, I'd let my forehead break the moist strands of its flickering web.

Then watched it flee into the ironweed, dissolving in the cluster of those purple stars

above. Allowing me to pass from *its* domain.

Revenge, perhaps? Arachnid's mark upon my brow, for something sensed, an attitude, within our righteous minds?

*Southwest Virginia*

## J.L. KUBICEK

# KNOW, AS EMILY

Sentences, in order,
with brevitas,
enabled *le mot juste*
to rest in her palm.
See, one fall, high
in the sky the departing "V"
and in their honking
the return of fire,
earth, water and ether
to their Olduval home
*wo die Zitronen bluhn;*
know, as Emily,
". . . the horse's heads
were toward eternity."

# ETERNAL TRAIL

Those who dance
to Greensleaves
may succumb
to Hercules dust
those who dance
to *Les Sylphides*
may succumb
to Lesbos dust,
equally rightful
as one journeys,
but once,
on the leaf
strewn trail
from the Olduval.

# CHRIS GORDON

# SHE WAS GOING TO EAT YOU ANYWAY

The white sow brought you three bees. Two of them caught fire and tainted honey. The third dances in reverse in circles in a cedar box small enough to fit in the space your eye, the left one, used to occupy before you tied it with threads to the collapsing stars in order to tell stories about places without perennial trees or relevant questions. Your sons ate honey. Now they're dead. In the evenings joy as the quality of light has been replaced by a rhythmic humming, beckoning the sow back from her fens. When she gets here open the box. Don't blame the bees. She was going to eat you anyway.

# WHIT HUBBARD

# THE DEATH OF POETRY


Poetry was born in a lime green field of daises strung up by
savages and crucified on a telephone pole
with power cables running through her ankles and wrists
and passengers from a moving train shooting her toes and
fingers

A child cut poetry down, dug her a shallow grave,
forgot to close her eyes when he rolled her in and at night
watched a pack of silhouetted wolves spread her remains
and in the morning saw vultures with their tire tread wings,
circle above

# DOUG RAMSPECK

# EPISTOLARY EVENING

Dear J____

The word was *vanish*, I believe, or maybe *cerulean*,
then suddenly you stopped, mid-breath, silenced
by a small song rising from the tupelos,
by the nasal courtship of a woodcock as it appeared
above us in the dusk sky, by the epistolary evening arranging
itself as orange glow, authoring its way
into the bottomlands.

And you told me the story of how your mother
used to write your father letters, mingled them
with the discarded skin
of a cottonmouth or an indigo, and bury them in the dense
loambeside the sweetgums in your back yard.
You told me how you imagined that the paper
in the letters was as pale as the insect larvae
that surely feasted on the words,
swallowed the words, excreted the words.

In *Letter of a Portuguese Nun,* you explain,
the French lover, Marquis de Chamilly, is the object
of such self-abandoned love that the words
burn as self-immolation on the page,
in the same way your mother would cut into the belly
of a pickerel frog to read its entrails, or would gather
epidendrums to place beneath her pillow
and thus write their way into her dreams.

In a final memory he is standing by the river.
*The river is a vowel*, you say.
And so he bends down to write a scratch
of beard against your cheek.
Your mother is weeping onto the page
in the remembered kitchen.
The page is wet as swamp.
And the shape of words disappears into the twilights.

# ANNE QUINNEY

# MALLARME'S DREAM

*Languages are imperfect because they multiply; the supreme language is missing. Inasmuch as thought consists of writing without pen and paper, without whispering even, without the sound of the immortal Word, the diversity of languages on earth meant that no one can utter words which would bear the miraculous stamp of truth herself incarnate."*

—Mallarmé

In announcing his dream "to paint, not the thing, but the effect it produces," Mallarmé radicalized poetic vision forever. If poetry once represented the literary tradition that, in revealing the essence of things with the help of language, believed itself to possess the capacity to seize what escapes our consciousness, Mallarmé offered a conception of poetry, not as the condensation of language, but as the vaporization of sounds. At a time when verse was in crisis, this crisis represented for him the occasion for the poet's voice to "be stilled and the initiative taken by the words themselves, which will be set in motion as they meet unequally in collision. And in an exchange of gleams they will flame out like glittering swaths of fire sweeping over precious stones, and thus replace the audible breathing in lyric poetry of old—replace the poet's own personal and passionate control of verse." He dreamed of creating in poetry an echo without an original enunciation, without a point of origin in a past time. He approached metaphysical questions in an elliptical fashion, through objects, while resisting their description. "Evoke an object little by little to show a state of mind (*un état d'âme*) or, conversely, choose an object and extract a state of mind from it by way of a series of decodings."

Far from being a poet who conceived the state of his own mind as a reflective mirror, Mallarmé did not try to decipher either objects or physical states, but suggested by means other than linguistic signification. In a much celebrated passage, the poet underscored his vision: "Naming objects suppresses three quarters of the delight of a poem which is created from the bliss of guessing little by little." He began by whitening the surface of the page and ended up by suggesting the possibility, not of self-representation, but of the evocation of this movement by which a poem is created and the poet, destroyed at the same time. Language functioned as an aid to touch the fleeting impression passing on the edge of consciousness. As he put it, "verse must not be composed of words, but of intentions, and all words are wiped out before sensation." Foreign, operating alone, language possesses an independent life that fascinated Mallarmé. He had a dream to give himself over to "the enchantment of creating (a poem) by the magic of rhyme" and this dream found its expression in his sonnet, "Se spurs ongles très-haut" (Her pure nails on high displaying their onyx").

Se spurs ongles très-haut...

Se spurs ongles très-haut dédiant leur onyx,
L'Angoisse, ce minuit, soutient, lampadophone,
Maint rêve vespéral brûlé par le Phénix
Que ne recueille pas de cinéraire amphore
Sur les crédences, au salon vide : nul ptyx,
Aboli bibelot d'inanité sonore,
(Car le Maître est allé puiser des pleurs au Styx
Avec ce seul objet don't le Néant s'honore.)

Mais proche la croisée au nord vacante, un or
Agonise selon peut-être le décor
Des licornes ruant du feu contre une nixe,

Elle, défunte nue en le miroir, encore
Que, dans l'oubli fermé par le cadre, se fixe
De scintillations sitôt le septuor

(Her pure nails on high displaying their onyx/ The lampbearer.
Anguish, at midnight sustains/ Those versperal dreams that are
burnt by the Phoenix/ And which no funeral amphora contains/
On credenzas in the empty room, no ptyx,/ Abolished knick-knack
of sonorous futility/ (For the Master has gone to draw tears from
the Styx/ With this sole object in which Nothingness takes pride.)
But in the vacant north, adjacent to the window panes, a shaft of
gold/ decays maybe along with the décor/ A nix sheathed in sparks
that a unicorn kicks./ Though she in the oblivion that the mirror
frames / Lies nude and defunct, there rains / the scintillations on
the one-and-six.)

This is the only poem Mallarmé wrote for which he envisioned
the possible illustration of "an *eau-forte* full of Dream and Void."
It would contain, he said, "an open nocturnal window, two attached
shutters, a room with no one in it, despite the still air and the
night made of absence and questioning, without furniture, except
the plausible etching about vague consolations, a frame, war-torn
and decaying, a mirror hanging in the back with its stellar and
incomprehensible reflection of Ursa Major that links the sky and
this dwelling abandoned by the world." Just as the word "void"
inscribes itself in the structure of this sonnet that twinkles with
words of absence, so does language become the sensual presence
of those absences. Between appearance and disappearance, the
space of the scene in "Se spurs ongles" is encumbered with words
that signify nothing, with interchangeable objects of vacuity, and
with physical "blanks." He gives us a series of synonyms for
Nothingness—"Those versperal dreams that are burnt," "the empty
room," "abolished knick-knack of sonorous futility," the "vacant
North," "nix," and the absent Master. A knick-knack is nothing
if not the garnish of emptiness. It refers to nothing in particular;
its role in the scene has less to do with its being "abolished" as it
aims to point itself as the thing so general that it suppresses all
things that can be known, identified with a sign. Its "sonorous

futility" reinforces the idea that silence here is as dense as the Nothingness is sonorous. Moreover the Master is absent, gone to fill the amphora with water that never existed.

Nothingness, emptiness, and absence circulate inexhaustively in the poem. Depleted of a story and of any action, the poem remains quiet in the sense that nothing happens and the space stays "full of void" in oxymoronic fashion. The necessary conditions for meaning are even absent. Thwarting the reader's need to invest the poem with meaning, Mallarmé fills the space with nonexistent objects so that the suppression of all references to the words allows for words themselves to create an effect. "Projected on the word: it's the inverse, I mean the meaning, if there is one in it is evoked by an internal mirage of words themselves. In allowing oneself to murmur it several times, one feels a rather cabalistic sensation." To be sure, language was the instrument of poetry for Mallarmé but he had another use for it. He wanted to show how a word has automatic existence apart from our ordinary use of it—hence his invention of the word "ptyx." In 1875, Adolph Racot told the story of Mallarmé who, while reading a sonnet at the salon at Leconte de Liède's home said, "I only needed something to rhyme with Styx; not finding one, I created a new musical instrument. Clearly, *ptyx* is odd since there is no such thing but it sounds good since it rhymes; and it is no less a vessel of futility since it never existed." Mallarmé tried in vain to explain that the word existed solely for its musical quality, yet critics of this poem strive to find the origins of this word. Perhaps it is Greek for "fold" or "crease" that opens up a whole field of interpretation around the richness of the word "fold" in Mallarmé's poetry. Or else it represents a mandolin that emits a recognized note or a shell inside of which one can hear the ocean.

If Mallarmé dreamt of exposing the limits of language as an illusion or a game, he nonetheless considered language to be an event of consciousness. Listening to the sounds of words, we believe in the reality behind them even if this reality is eclipsed at the moment of articulation. "Thus, in reading, a lonely quiet concert is given for our minds, and they in turn, less noisily reach its meaning. Poetry, accompanied by the Idea, is the ultimate Music, and cannot be anything else." Every word gains its value in the melody of which it is a part and consequently, every word disappears as an individual element. The reader's task is to unify these elements according to a concretely defined translation as if a "secret," a Mallarméan tomb, were buried at its center. Poetry does not ask to be understood, however, according to Mallarmé's dream. The sound effects become more important than the sense of meaning. This strategy to create poetry against representation is evident in the objects that do not correspond to real things, for example, "the nail's onyx" or "ptyx." The "Nothingness" (*Le Néant*) of the poem remains the only one to take pride in these objects; while the reader automatically puts himself on the trail of signs as soon as he begins the first line. We cannot help ourselves, said Mallarmé: "We dream of words brilliant at once in meaning and sound or darkening in meaning as in sound, luminously and elementally self-succeeding. *But*, let us remember that if our dream were fulfilled, *verse would not exist* — verse, which, in all its wisdom, atones for the sins of languages, comes nobly to their aid."

Certain contemporary readers hold that poetry never stops speaking of itself and of the difficulties of written expression, especially when it speaks most clearly of another subject. We say that it is the thematic opacity that disguises the fact that a poem is concerned with nothing if not language. With Mallarmé, the suspicion towards representation is present from the moment that a poem begins to speak. Insisting on giving meaning to verse and following the thread of his thoughts throughout his work forces us to situate the poet, Mallarmé, within his words. It is the same impulse that drives the reader to trace certain key images that appear at several points in his poems in order to construct the personality of Mallarmé. We search for a system of references and an author (*auteurite*) in a habitual and unavoidable fashion. Nevertheless, the literary space belongs to no one. According to Mallarmé, "not personified, this volume of writing, as much as one separates from it as the author, does not beg the reader's eye. So, you know, between human accessories, it happens on its own: done, being." Nowhere is the subject coherent and whole. Instead the "immortal word" floats without a body, taking shape in the vacant and absent objects named. "The Orphic explanation of the earth" and the affirmation of the absence occur when the poet splits into a million pieces while he reveals blinding things. "Though she in the oblivion that the mirror frames / Lies nude and defunct, there rains / the scintillations of the one-and-six." Even the defunct nude tries to stabilize her reflection in the mirror only to recover there an alphabet of white stars against the vast night sky.

Mallarmé's quest for a balanced creation in which words mutually illuminate and enrich each other manifests itself in the musical suspension at the end of each line. "Everything becomes suspense, a fragmentary arrangement with alternation and opposition, concurring with the total rhythm, this would be the poem silenced, in the blanks, in a way, by each penditive." The author is anonymous and the reader must confront the negation of the subject and the erasure of the object. Thanks to music, poetry retains an enigma the astonishing effect of which is its goal. The poet's ideas, as "gestures" of the word, become in the future a kind of "mandolin" in Mallarmé's terms. In other words, sounds that are analogous to things make echoes resound in the text, not of the poet, but of their assembly that never ceases to murmur. In the hands of the reader lies the book that "will try to suffice, to open up the interior scene and make the echoes whisper from within it."

# CONTRIBUTORS

KAYE VOIGT ABIKHALED is a *VOX* contributor.

VERA ARTI was born in Russia in 1961.  She lives and writes in Oxford, Mississippi.

ANNA BAKER lives and writes in Oxford, Mississippi.  She has most recently been published in *Arkansas Review, Atlanta Review,* and *VOX.*

F.J. BERGMANN is to blame for *madpoetry.org* and *fibitz.com.*  She lacks literary academic credentials, but is kind to those so afflicted.  Her work has appeared in *Beloit Poetry Review Journal, Cannibal, Diagram, Malleable Jangle,* and two chapbooks, *Sauce Robert* (Pavement Saw) and *Regia* (Parallel Press).

VALERIE BRUSOV was born and died in Moscow.  He was one of the most well known Russian "Silver Age" symbolists poets.  His goal was to build a Russian symbolist poetic school based on French symbolist poetic achievements, and to become a leader of it.

ZACHARY C. BUSH, 23, is a writer of poetry, fiction, personal essay, and magazine features.  He is work has appeared in over a dozen literary journals.

SUSAN V. CARLOS has published in *Xavier Review, Cotyledon, Avocet* and others.  She lives and writes in Houma, Louisiana.

MITCH COHEN has an MFA from The University of Iowa creative writing program.  He lives and writes in Oxford, Mississippi.

NANCY DEVINE teaches high school English in Grand Forks, North Dakota.  She co-directs the Red River Valley Writing Project, a local site of the National Writing Project.  Her poems have appeared recently in *Main Channel Voices* and *Matter 9 Fuel.*

FRANKIE DRAYUS recently graduated from the MFA program at New York University.  Her poems and fiction appear in *Third Coast, Passages North,* and *Barrow Street.*  She lives in Los Angles.

CLIFFORD PAUL FETTERS is a *VOX* contributor.

ERIC RAANAN FISCHMAN is a graduating senior at Hunter College in New York where he majors in Creative Writing and minors in Media.  His work has appeared in *Shampoo, Confused Muse, The Hiss Quarterly, Twenty3Magazine, Margin,* Hunter College's *The Olive Tree Review,* among others.

BARBARA CLAIRE FREEMAN is a professor of literature at University of California, Berkeley.  Her poetry has appeared in *The Boston Review, The Colorado Review, The Harvard Review, The Iowa Review,* among others.

# CONTRIBUTORS

CAROL FRITH's books include *In and out of Light* (Bacchae Press) and *Never enough Zeros* (Palanquin Press). She is co-editor of *Ekphrasis.*

RYAN FOX lives in Charlottesville, Virginia. You can find his poems in recent or forthcoming issues of *Iowa Review, New Orleans Review, Caketrain,* and *Columbia.*

CHRIS GORDON has published in *Hunger Magazine, Northwest Review, Fence,* and others. His translations have appeared in *Modern Haiku* and *Circumference.*

JOHN HARVEY's poems have appeared in *Gulf Coast, The Paris Review, Whiskey Island, XCP* and other journals. He is Resident Playwright with the Mildred's Umbrella Theater Company, and his new play *ROT* runs this February into March at the Gremillion.

WAYNE HOGAN's cartoons have appeared in *The Quarterly* and other magazines and journals. He lives in Clarksville, Tennessee.

ARTHUR E. HOWELLS II is editor of Rancid Beast Press. He lives and writes in Phoenix, Arizona.

J.L. KUBICEK is a *VOX* contributor.

RENZO LLORENTE teaches philosophy on Saint Louis University's Madrid campus. His articles on ethics, Marxism. 19th-century German philosophy and other topics have been published in a variety of academic journals.

SHAD MARSH has published poetry in *Artvoice, Ghoti, Light, The Muse, The Pebble Lake Review, VOX,* and other journals.

MARGOT MILLER holds a PhD. in French literature. Her creative work has appeared in *ChickFlicks, Subtle Tea, Fringe, Steel City Review, Toasted Cheese,* and others.

GEORGE MOORE is a VOX contributor.

BENJAMIN MORRIS is a native of Mississippi but now lives in Cambridge, England, where he is a Ph. D. candidate in archaeology. His poetry and prose have been recognized in both the US and the UK.

MAURICE OLIVER has published in *Bullfight Review, One Forty Two Magazine, Stride Magazine, Potomac Review,* and others. He lives and writes in Portland, Oregon.

CHRIS PASCO-PRANGER lives and writes in Oxford, Mississippi.

LEIGH PHILLIPS is a doctoral student at Binghamton University. Her poetry has been published in *Longshot, Lodestar Quarterly, Harpur Palette, Beautiful Poems: An Anthology of Fusion,* among others.

# CONTRIBUTORS

DEREK POLLARD is an associate editor at New Issues Poetry and Prose and a contributing editor at Barrow Street. His poems and reviews appear or are forthcoming in *580 Split, Colorado Review, Court Green, Interim*, and *Quarterly West*, among others.

GISÈLE PRASSINOS (Born 1920) is a French writer associated with the surrealist movement. Her writing was discovered by André Breton in 1934, when she was just fourteen, and published in the French surrealist magazine *Minotaure*. Her first book *La Sauterelle arthritique* (*The Arthritic Grasshopper*) was published in 1935 with a preface by Paul Eluard and a photograph by Man Ray.

ANNE QUINNEY is an Associate Professor of French in the Department of Modern Languages at The University of Mississippi. She received her Ph.D in French Studies from Duke University in 2000 and holds a master's from The Universite de Paris VIII and a B.A. from Brown University. Her publications include the translation of French psychoanalyst JB Pontalis' memoir, *Windows* (Lincoln: University of Nebraska Press, 2003) and articles in *Contemporary French & Francophone Studies: Sites, The South Central Review, Dalhousie French Studies, The Translator*, and other journals.

DOUG RAMSPECK'S poems have been published by more than 150 journals including *West Branch, Rattle, Confrontation Magazine, Connecticut Review, Rosebud, Nimrod, Seneca Review, RHINO*, and *Cream City Review*.

MARY BARRES RIGGS, was a professional ballet dancer in New York and Europe, performing under the direction of Bronislava Nijinska and Hans Brenna of the Royal Danish Ballet. She holds degrees from Harvard, Ole Miss, and the University of Utah. She teaches yoga and writes interdisciplinary essays on dance and music with her husband Dr.Robert Riggs.

DENNIS SALEH lives and writes in Seaside, California.

G. DAVID SCHWARTZ is the author of *A Jewish Appraisal of Dialogue*. His latest book is entitled *Midrash*.

JEAN-MARK SENS holds a Ph. D. from the University of Southern Mississippi. His most recent book *Appetite* was published by Red Hen Press.

ANDREW SHELLEY was educated at Oxford and Cambridge. His books include *Peaceworks* (The Many Press) and *Requiem* (Spectacular Diseases).

PETER SPECKER has published poetry in *Amelia, California State Quarterly, Pegasus, Margie, Indiana Review*, among others. He lives in Los Angeles and Ithaca, New York.

DANA STAMPS II has published in *Iconoclast, THEMA, American Dissident, Blue Unicorn, Phineas, Avocet*, as well as others.

# CONTRIBUTORS

JUDITH STRASSER's poetry collection, *The Reason Unreason Project* won the Lewis-Clark Expedition Award and will be published in 2007. She is also the author of a memoir, *Black Eye: Escaping a Marriage, Writing a Life*, and co-editor of the anthology *On Retirement: 75 Poems*.

DAN SRYK teaches world literature and creative writing at Virginia Intermont College in Bristol, and is the author of five collections of poems and prose parables, including *The Artistand the Crow* (Purdue University Press), and two new collections, *Dimming Radiance* (Wind Publications 2007) and *Solace of the Aging Mare* (The Mid-America Press 2008), are forth-coming. His most recent poems and prose pieces are appearing in such publications as *Atlanta Review, Ploughshares, Boulevard*, and *North American Review.*

JASON TANDON is the author of two chapbooks, *Flight* (Finishing Line Press, forthcoming 2007) and *Rumble Strip* (sunnyoutside). His first full-length collection, *Give over the Heckler*, was a finalist for the 2006 Kinereth Gensler Award from Alice James Books.

MARK TERRILL's books include *The United Colors of Death* (Pathway Press), *Bread and Fish* (The Figures), and *Here to Learn*: *Remembering Paul Bowles* (Green Bean Press). He has lived in Germany since 1984.

IAN WILLIAMS teaches American literature in Massachusetts and co-edits *Misunderstandings Magazine*. His poetry and fiction have appeared or are forthcoming in *Pebble Lake Review, MARGIE, Callaloo*, and *Descant*.

*VOX*

*The New Avant Garde*

OUTHOUSE OF THE APRIL (CRUELEST MONTH) MOON.